Britten Experienced

Who writes the books we read about music that excites us, and why? Is 'classical music' all about class? Related questions underpin this partly polemical study, written by an academic who believes that the Humanities, to be really humane, must confront their methods and aims. Two recent studies of Benjamin Britten have specifically interested the author, who was educated in a world where the composer was a living subject of criticism and praise, his works reflecting values, worries and dramas that were not just about 'music'. Franklin's response is to question the recent writers, proposing that, like theirs, his own story conditioned when and how he experienced Britten. This he unfolds autobiographically in and around the discussion of specific works. Recalling his encounters with the composer as a schoolboy, as a student and opera-goer, and then as a teacher, he challenges recent assertions about Britten and modernism in the period.

Peter Franklin, a professor of music at the University of Oxford until 2014, is an Emeritus Fellow of St Catherine's College. He has taught on both sides of the Atlantic and has written a number of books and articles on Mahler, Schreker and other composers of the period c. 1880–1933.

Britten Experienced
Modernism, Musicology and Sentiment

Peter Franklin

LONDON AND NEW YORK

First published 2024
by Routledge
4 Park Square, Milton Park, Abingdon, Oxon OX14 4RN

and by Routledge
605 Third Avenue, New York, NY 10158

Routledge is an imprint of the Taylor & Francis Group, an informa business

© 2024 Peter Franklin

The right of Peter Franklin to be identified as author of this work has been asserted in accordance with sections 77 and 78 of the Copyright, Designs and Patents Act 1988.

All rights reserved. No part of this book may be reprinted or reproduced or utilised in any form or by any electronic, mechanical, or other means, now known or hereafter invented, including photocopying and recording, or in any information storage or retrieval system, without permission in writing from the publishers.

Trademark notice: Product or corporate names may be trademarks or registered trademarks, and are used only for identification and explanation without intent to infringe.

British Library Cataloguing-in-Publication Data
A catalogue record for this book is available from the British Library

Library of Congress Cataloging-in-Publication Data
Names: Franklin, Peter, author.
Title: Britten experienced : modernism, musicology and sentiment / Peter Franklin. Description: [1.] | Abingdon, Oxon ; New York : Routledge, 2024. | Includes bibliographical references and index.
Identifiers: LCCN 2023059132 | ISBN 9781032666600 (hardback) | ISBN 9781032666648 (paperback) | ISBN 9781032666631 (ebook)
Subjects: LCSH: Britten, Benjamin, 1913–1976—Criticism and interpretation. | Music—20th century—History and criticism. | Opera—20th century. | Modernism (Music)
Classification: LCC ML410.B853 F73 2024 | DDC 780.92—dc23/ eng/20231226
LC record available at https://lccn.loc.gov/2023059132

ISBN: 978-1-032-66660-0 (hbk)
ISBN: 978-1-032-66664-8 (pbk)
ISBN: 978-1-032-66663-1 (ebk)

DOI: 10.4324/9781032666631

Typeset in Times New Roman
by Apex CoVantage, LLC

Contents

Foreword		*vii*
List of Figures		*x*
1	**Introduction: The Roots of My Musical Taste and Chowrimootoo's Worry**	1
	'Noye's Fludde' from the Pews 8	
2	**Secondary-School Britten: *The Turn of the Screw***	15
	Music A-level and 'War Requiem' 21	
3	**Encountering Britten as a Music Student at York in the Late 1960s**	27
	Essay: Grimes *and the Sentimental 33*	
4	**Graduation: Britten and Pears Return to York**	46
	Essay: Billy Budd*: Confronting the Highbrow Critique of Opera 47*	
5	**Singing at Aldeburgh: Musical Scholarship**	54
	Opera in the '70s and Death in Venice *57*	
6	**A Trip to East Berlin and the Start of a Career**	68
	Teaching Opera. Britten's Death. Mahler and Donald Mitchell 70	

7 **Essay: Travels. Towards Musical Meaning (The *Serenade for Tenor, Horn and Strings*)** Leeds. 'The Open Secret'. Philip Brett and 'A Midsummer Night's Dream' 85	78
8 **Essay: Modernism and Musicology**	100
Select Bibliography	*110*
Acknowledgements	*112*
Index	*113*

Foreword

Academics working in 'the Humanities' are keenly aware that ours is an age of Science and scientists. Confronted by planetary disaster and pandemics, we know that we must contemplate with care what and why we do what we do. Many scientists, of course, readily value their Arts colleagues' curation of and contribution to 'culture', or even 'what makes us human', but such well-intended phrases conceal, we may suspect (and even understand), residual suspicion of the apparently rudderless musings of non-performer academics on the intellectual side of the Humanities. Those who are open to self-criticism – as most of us surely are – have consequently sought to appropriate and learn from the academic culture of our scientist colleagues. This is detected in something like the practice of musicological analysis, and in the more historical and evaluative enterprises of tracing, cataloguing and describing that go back to the foundational work of Guido Adler, the modern discipline's notional founder in late nineteenth-century Vienna. Aspects of the presentational methods and practice of both scientific and historical scholarship have long been self-imposed, like those requiring workers in a shared field carefully to cite and reference each other. We clearly *need* each other for mutual support beyond the normal requirements of academic neighbourliness. Career progression and the survival of departments can depend upon such support and the interest (which may of course entail criticism) of a wider scholarly community upon whose cohesiveness its collective survival depends; we still admit that it is the scientists who must solve the larger survival questions, in the more apocalyptic sense, where our own efforts and preoccupations might indeed appear more decorative than decisive.

The downside of current academic practice is marked by the Humanities' special susceptibility to forms of strategic misunderstanding and even hypocrisy, not least within individual disciplines like musicology. Citing and referencing other scholars for more political or housekeeping reasons than convinced esteem for their contribution might be an example. A kind of informal colonialism can infect such 'political' references. Colleagues may be cited (often rather pointlessly) as having 'noted' something the present writer is (we take it) in the process of more eloquently and perceptively outlining. The noted are rarely granted evidential proof that their cited book or article has been studied as a complete argument, as an evolving whole whose business may not just be to offer referential corroboration for colleagues in the spirit of 'together we stand'; a significant number are left to fall into difficult-to-access 'Endnotes' or – worse – an entry in the Bibliography.

I raise this matter out of a sense of personal responsibility here, and with the recent, dauntingly monumental example of J. P. E. Harper-Scott's *Ideology in Britten's Operas* before me.[1] I will inevitably refer to it from time to time, returning to engage further with it at the end of the present study. It stands as an example and warning to us all in its dual character as a manifesto for what a critical musicology might be and do and a kind of professional suicide-note from a colleague who had grown terminally angry about the discipline and contemporary humanistic academia in general and has now left the profession altogether. Meanwhile, in what follows my careful reading (I hope) of Christopher Chowrimootoo's book *Middlebrow Modernism: Britten's Operas and the Great Divide*[2] might on occasion appear to demonstrate its own form of questionable competitive superiority. What I want to say is in large measure dependent upon that book and its carefully researched reception history of Britten's operas by critics affiliated to modernist taste and principles. These underpinned the established (and possibly mythical?) musicological understanding of what was once considered the kind of Twentieth-Century Music that 'mattered'. The value of Chowrimootoo's book in this respect is considerable, but having followed my recommended principle and attended carefully to the full unfolding and presentational character of its argument, I have found things that I want to question, in terms of what their contribution might be to the larger project of the Humanities in the twenty-first century. I am both cited and footnoted in his text but find myself on occasion wanting to say more, inspired – called forth, as it were – to speak from the reliquary-chapel of footnotes in which I find myself. Perhaps, like Titurel from his niche in *Parsifal*, I raise a quivering hand to confess that something asserted of a cultural past in which I participated, as a consumer of the music Chowrimootoo writes about, feels wrong – that it was not quite like that. I am moved at these points to ask if his project is in fact *proposing* something, articulating a critical view – here of Britten's music – that might be as much his as that of the contemporary critics he cites, which is perfectly permissible. The totality of his book has interested me as much as its valuably amassed historical material.

In trying to discern its underlying purpose and position – which I hope I have engaged with as something more important and perhaps more disturbing than just another source of things to 'note' – I have found myself wanting to say other and different things about Britten and his operas, and my relationship with him, and them, as a seeker after musical knowledge, pleasure, inspiration and sometimes sympathy. In the spirit, perhaps, of Britten-scholar Philip Rupprecht's observation that "all art is new art, and all art is local,"[3] my approach bypasses many of the sanctioned modes of musicological discourse and enquiry. Perhaps it escapes them in the way that malicious variants of the coronavirus might escape the action of our cherished vaccines. Perhaps I am simply seeking the 'humanity' in this particular branch of the Humanities. If I have stumbled across any, it is thanks to Chowrimootoo's attempt to confront something in his book which itself underpins and drives his (to me) less congenial arguments. I nevertheless acknowledge these as my inspiration for what follows. This study seeks ultimately to respond, albeit in gentler and perhaps more modest fashion, to the demanding *cri-de-coeur* of Harper-Scott's book, where he laments that disciplinary attention "has gradually been deflected away from the human self-knowing that has always been at the heart of musical encounters."[4]

A Note On the Text

The decision to respond to Chowrimootoo's book in a form of autobiographical narrative arose from a curiously personal statement he makes at the outset of his book. It subsequently disappears from sight but feels enigmatically, somehow actively, present 'behind' his text. I have consequently sought to be clear about the context, background and personal underpinning of my own thoughts about Britten in response to those of Chowrimootoo and (to me) the more sympathetic, if also more demanding, Harper-Scott (who similarly draws upon his own experience). My text consequently moves between autobiographical accounts of my own contemporary engagement with Britten's music and four 'ideas'-based essays. The essays seek to challenge and contribute to the critique of certain key works. The essays have more formal headings, indicating their content, and are focal points of the book. They follow the timeline of its autobiographical sections, upon which they draw and whose presence they are intended to help explain. The text as a whole might often seem more 'novelistic' than 'musicological' in attempting to engage the reader in its underlying argument about the discipline, leading towards a final knitting together of that argument and the autobiography. This is intended and integral to its aim.

Notes

1 J.P.E. Harper-Scott, *Ideology in Britten's Operas* (Cambridge: Cambridge University Press, 2018).
2 Christopher Chowrimootoo, *Middlebrow Modernism. Britten's Opera and the Great Divide* (Oakland, California: University of California Press, 2018).
3 Philip Rupprecht, *British Musical Modernism. The Manchester Group and their Contemporaries* (Cambridge: Cambridge University Press, 2015/17), 451.
4 Harper-Scott, *Ideology in Britten's Operas*, 176.

Figures

2.1 The two central pages of the Sadler's Wells programme for *The Turn of the Screw* on 7th November 1962.   19
3.1 Title page of the Sadlers Wells programme for *Peter Grimes* on 11th April 1967.   28
3.1a The cast list from the programme for the April 1967 *Peter Grimes*.   29
7.1 A black-and-white reproduction of the ENO Programme cover for Christopher Alden's 2011 production of *A Midsummer Night's Dream*.   93

1 Introduction: The Roots of My Musical Taste and Chowrimootoo's Worry

Perhaps I should describe this somewhat polemical memoir of a composer I never knew (although I once briefly met him in person and saw him many times) as a memoir of a composer I came to *feel* I knew. As a consumer and later teacher of his music, I grew up in a post-war world that he, and it, enhanced and influenced in numerous ways. My own entry into the particular world of what has haphazardly come to be bundled together as 'classical music' (a term from which I recoil) had nevertheless been some kind of an accident, almost a mistake. The fact that 'serious' music, as we might also have called it in the 1950s and '60s, was part of the upper- or upper-middle-class-world to which those of us brought up in the dreary outer suburbs of London were somehow, even subliminally, encouraged to aspire might not necessarily have recommended it. But at that time I was far from being a rebellious type. My desire to escape was open to all means that presented themselves.

A favourite uncle, my mother's closest brother, was our nearest link to that world and its serious music. He had gone early into the army from a post-school office job and served in India in the Second World War before returning to make his way, without a degree, slowly up the ladder of the legal profession until he ended up with cases of his own in a prominent firm of solicitors in London. One might have seen it as a mark of his success that he possessed a fine and much-polished early 1960s 'radiogram'. It not only played but also housed his cherished collection of Beethoven symphonies beside his wife's records of songs from the shows. He would often play us a movement of one or another of the symphonies after a Saturday tea, before the four of us – my parents, my sister and me – would pile into the car to drive back from Hounslow to our rather similar, if less tidily kept, pebble-dash semi-detached house in Wembley (our uncle and aunt were childless). Musical taste in our house had hitherto been dominated by Children's Favourites on the wireless; we had enjoyed the popular and novelty songs of Danny Kaye, Max Bygraves and others in the 1950s. By the time my sister was buying Elvis Presley singles ('Return to Sender' was played incessantly for a time) I had passed through Russ Conway to Winifred Atwell and 'Sparky's Magic Piano' – reluctant though I was as an elementary pianist (put to it initially by my mother). My

DOI: 10.4324/9781032666631-1

2 The Roots of My Musical Taste and Chowrimootoo's Worry

own laborious playing was far from magical, but those performers and recordings had chanced to introduce me to music of the more serious, longer-winded kind for which my father had a partly buried taste. He once bought himself an LP of Tchaikovsky's First Piano Concerto and had a sneaking susceptibility to Puccini and *Madama Butterfly*. The three vinyl discs of that opera he would load reverentially onto the tall 'auto-change' spindle of our family record player (portable and far less grand than our uncle's radiogram, for all that we gave it a table of its own). The discs would drop down and play, one by one, taking us through the first half of the opera, often while my father and I were doing our best with interior decoration jobs like papering walls and ceilings, before the records had to be turned over for the second half.

My mother's contribution, eclectic though her tastes could be, was a more direct and enthusiastic embrace of the 'shows'. They were mostly American musicals, sometimes British in subject matter (*My Fair Lady*), but Rogers and Hammerstein's *The King and I* and (best of all) *South Pacific* were favourites. Emile de Becque's 'This Nearly Was Mine', from the latter, became an early model of powerfully moving emotional expression in music that was linked, in an apparently seamless way, to my growing passion for Tchaikovsky. That dominated my teens and led to frequent expeditions into London on the Piccadilly Line to Thursday evening 'Tchaikovsky nights' at the Royal Albert Hall. A friend and I would worshipfully admire and feel ourselves to have been (as we were) profoundly moved by the Violin Concerto, the later symphonies or the '1812' Overture, in which the orchestra would be reinforced by a uniformed military band and 'cannon effects'.

In jest, my early acceptance of my sexual identity as queer (the term 'gay' had yet to acquire currency) might seem now to illuminate my intemperate devotion to musical and theatrical explorations of dramatized emotional experience. At that time, before I found myself being unsuccessfully trained (rebelliousness then ignited) to consider such devotion as a mark of 'sentimentality, 'self-indulgence', 'romanticism', 'Kitsch' or whatever, the interconnection of these forms appeared self-evident. The works that our school music teacher played to us on a portable record player (theoretically perhaps the worst possible approach to music education, avoiding the need to prepare for systematic teaching) bored many of my contemporaries as much as they flung open windows to me. These revealed mindscapes of imaginative emotional discourse and visionary luxuriance that were like interplanetary journeys away from the dullness of our repressed suburban world of endlessly repeating roads of similar houses and endless pavements from which only summer holidays, the TV and the Piccadilly Line provided escape. Elgar's *Pomp and Circumstance* marches, 'Mars' from Holst's *Planets*, even the Brahms's *St Anthony Chorale* Variations (vaguely 'followed' on a wide-format Penguin score that I treasured) seemed to provide a direct link to experiences and to places that were part of a 'wider world' we otherwise glimpsed in American TV series or news bulletins at a time when foreign travel, for us, was as fantastic an imagined possibility as flying off on the magic carpet of Christmas pantomimes.

The Roots of My Musical Taste and Chowrimootoo's Worry

My eventual arrival at the University of York as a novice music student and newly re-committed pianist in 1966 brought me suddenly and rather unexpectedly into an environment that seemed open to, and even a part of that wider world. Close to York's picturesque medieval walls, in the centre of town, Wilfrid Mellers would mesmerize us in lectures that were themselves like incantatory confirmations and explorations of the intensities and significance of all that I had suspected about 'serious' music. But his and the department's laudable devotion not only to performance but also *composition*, as an activity in which we were all to participate, introduced us to the new aesthetic politics of a free or 'modernist' creativity. This was inspired by innovatory refusal to be bound by the conventions of classical music in its more repressive, ideological guise (not something I had previously grasped or been troubled by). That creative rebellion in turn generated its own no less repressive politics of fashion, quasi-moralistic partialities and rejections that had little time for much of the music that I had hitherto found so welcoming to the inner needs and aspirations of my teenage years. Where my Beethovenian uncle had once openly avowed his distaste for "Benjamin Britten and all *that* kind of thing" (nonetheless buying me the score of *The Young Person's Guide to the Orchestra* that I had eagerly requested for my 15th birthday in 1962), by the late '60s and early '70s I found many of my contemporaries enthusiastically sharing his distaste, while echoing the party line of some of their more recently arrived 'experimental' composition teachers. For them Britten and Shostakovich were confusingly "not even *composers*" by any definition acceptable to them. Those others to whom I was then most strongly drawn, like Wagner, Mahler, Strauss and Sibelius (particularly Mahler, to whom my doctoral dissertation would later be devoted) might best be tolerated as 'anticipating' the legitimate modernists represented by Schoenberg and the Second Viennese School. Stravinsky, Hindemith and Weill were more vaguely and uneasily drawn into the charmed circle of New Music at whose centre figures like Pierre Boulez, Karlheinz Stockhausen and John Cage were enshrined as exemplary pioneers of the New.

By that time, as will have become evident, Britten's music was part of my inner landscape, but in ways that have yet to be fully explained. For the moment it will suffice to note the curious misalignment of my Beethovenian uncle's rejection of Britten as a representative of disagreeable modernism, with that of my 1970s colleagues and certain of their teachers (not Mellers) whose embrace of the New Music entailed no less definitive a rejection of Britten (along with Shostakovich), but for quite different reasons. Here I must turn to the book whose role in prompting this memoir I have already confessed.

* * *

That Britten defied straightforward classification in the 1960s and after is undoubtedly revealing not only of musical but also other cultural rifts and oppositions at that time. It was not just a matter of cerebral modernism *versus* popular music – since the latter category was itself riven by innumerable sub-categorical distinctions, beside that larger one distinguishing the thriving industry of commercial 'pop' music from the differently popular, perhaps differently 'classed' classical music of the kind that my first secondary-school music teacher used to play to us. That was mostly the music of late-Victorian and Edwardian England, its imperial and traditionalist baggage innocently ungrasped by me – although challenged and questioned by other, already out-of-fashion but still relatively popular composers like Delius and Vaughan Williams. The anti-English stance of the former in some way complemented the half-concealed anti-establishment orientation of the latter, who had nevertheless been much used by the BBC during the Second World War as the guardian of a comforting sort of pastoral 'Englishness' that unquestionably raised in its own way the spectre of national difference and oppositions.[1] Such oppositions were notoriously institutionalized by Germany under the Third Reich, which even appeared confusingly to honour Vaughan Williams when he was awarded the Shakespeare Prize of the University of Hamburg in 1937.[2] This highlighted from the wings, as it were, a raft of key questions about difference and legitimacy between the merely 'consumed' and the ideologically 'imposed' when it came either to national identity or the opposition to any kind of popular appeal by those wedded to the stern rigours of cerebral modernism in its implicit, or (later) explicit embrace of anti-authoritarian revolutionary morality and politics (as implied in the writing of Third Reich refugee Theodor Adorno).

All of this has been negotiated in different ways in three valuable critical and historical contributions to Britten studies that have appeared in the last decade, beginning with Heather Wiebe's *Britten's Unquiet Pasts: Sound and Memory in Postwar Reconstruction* in 2012; its careful contextual archaeology illuminated what she generously describes as "a set of works . . . that grappled in especially subtle ways with the problem of building musical culture in the wartime and postwar years, addressing the ideas of community, ritual and the deep English past."[3] This was followed in 2018 by the differently critical engagement with Britten's operas of J. P. E. Harper-Scott, in *Ideology in Britten's Operas*.[4] In the very same year there appeared the third of these studies, and the one that will most frequently engage me here. As soon as I began to read the Acknowledgements (one often feels such things are designed to be skipped, or left to be read at some future time) I was glad that I had, being struck by the fact that Christopher Chowrimootoo should have opened the book he provocatively titled *Middlebrow Modernism: Britten's Operas and the Great Divide* by postponing questions about historical context, preferring boldly to personalize and even internalize the issues at stake in a striking opening sentence:

> Those who know me well know that beneath my austere, modernist exterior resides a sentimentality as sickly as anything in *Peter Grimes*.[5]

The Roots of My Musical Taste and Chowrimootoo's Worry 5

Know *me*, the ostensibly austere modernist author declares, and you will know that my own position is potentially compromised by 'sentimentality'. This is further defined as 'sickly' in that striking, question-begging suggestion that its sickliness is somehow matched by equivalent levels of compromised 'sentimentality' in Britten's most widely acclaimed opera. Acclaimed, that is, perhaps by *you*, dear reader, who might therefore need to bow before the apparent healthiness of the modernist austerity that will be exercised in the critical study of selected operas that follows (in this he echoes the sterner didactic conviction of Harper-Scott's book).

As one of those who might want to whisper an admonishing 'Hang on a minute!', while preparing to be shamed by Chowrimootoo's evidently careful research and analysis of negative contemporary responses to Britten, I must raise at least a tentative question about some of the critics through whom he appears to ventriloquize his evidently ambivalent attitude to Britten's own "ambivalence and duplicity" as he describes it (on page 16). I am thinking of commentators like Robin Holloway, who in the mid-1960s was (not unlike Tippett and others before him) legitimately staking out a position as a rival younger-generation contemporary composer (b. 1943), envious of Britten's annoyingly continued success and apparent popularity. Assumptions derived too boldly from such selected corners of reception history may find themselves compromised by other kinds of historical evidence. Chowrimootoo shows awareness of this when, in his chapter on *Peter Grimes*, having identified "sentimental melodies" in its musical fabric, an unspoken but surely highly germane nervousness about what that epithet 'sentimental' really *means* leads him rhetorically to assure us that the fifth interlude in *Grimes* (the Prelude to Act III) "would have been considered sentimental by 'new' realists of Britten's own time."[6]

No examples are given, nor individuals named who might have called themselves 'new realists'. I confess that I never recall hearing that term used in the 1960s, although in all fairness I *would* be prepared to cite some possibly corroborating examples from "Britten's own time." I might reference an English composer who, whatever he would have called himself in the early 1930s, resoundingly criticized a Greta Garbo film he had recently seen as "violently and sickeningly sentimental." Another, who detested Vaughan Williams's music and thought Elgar "imperialist," even validated the main title of Chowrimootoo's study when mocking traditionalist music critics in 1951:

> luckily they don't really affect the public much – only those dreary middlebrows who don't know what to think till they read the *New Statesman*!

The questions and problems raised by Chowrimootoo's cautiously argued and carefully researched study are brought into focus when I point out that my unnamed voices from "Britten's own time" were in fact those of Britten himself, in both instances.[7]

6   The Roots of My Musical Taste and Chowrimootoo's Worry

By moving Britten out of the implicitly victimized position of a 'case' into that of a participant in the cultural oppositions and debates that Chowrimootoo is interested in, the wider potential of his project, as an historical study comparable to Wiebe's, is revealed. It hardly needed to be an *ad hominem*, and rather personal, critical examination of this one composer from the single, and (I am bound to suggest) period perspective of mid-twentieth-century modernist scorn of all that was 'other' than austere, unsentimental, un-tonal, unpopular – a perspective that, as we have seen, Britten himself well understood. He adopted his own version of it when contemplating Elgar, Vaughan Williams, Sibelius and Walton in his younger days. By over-investing in the critical and contextually rather specific historical category of 'middlebrow' as if it usefully defined creative strategies, Chowrimootoo nevertheless succeeds in bringing back to life an historical and critical debate within culture (meaning relatively 'high' British musical culture). At the same time he appears to disable the wider historical value of his project by investing over much in one of its examined viewpoints in order, as it were, to agree with Britten's negative critics and to marginalize (as middlebrow, *New Statesmanly*?) the voices of his supporters in such a way as to generate 'period' critiques of his works that are historically coherent but conceptually and responsively limited by what he himself presents at the outset as that specifically personal problem that he has with 'sentimentality'. Its association with 'sickness' and psychological infirmity he seems anxious to emphasize for reasons that appear, indeed, to reinscribe the socio-cultural partialities of those very musical modernists whose Terminal Prestige was long since diagnosed by Susan McClary,[8] as has been their peculiarly British manifestation by Dai Griffiths in an entertaining article, pointedly entitled 'On Grammar-Schoolboy Music'.[9]

I write of these things (echoing Jacob Bronowski's long-ago response to a Parkinson TV interview question[10]) 'with a full heart' because "Britten's own time" was also latterly *my* own time. I remember the debates about Britten, just as I remember experiencing his music as the debates unfolded. In what follows, I seek not simply to criticize but perhaps to take Chowrimootoo's lead and add to his a differently personalized account of some of the operas whose reception he examines, as of other works experienced by the middle-class, presumably middle*brow*, and suburban, first-generation university student that I was in York in the late 1960s. I was almost inevitably goaded into responding to the 'modernist' aesthetic that grew eager to devalue a lot of the music with which Wilfrid Mellers himself inspired us to engage. There was someone for whom Chowrimootoo's 'sentimentality' might have been more generously, if somewhat ostentatiously, defined as humane emotional sensitivity to music invoking both the modern, post-Renaissance expressive and communicative conceits of 'incarnation' and what Mellers described as the older, less conventionally harmonious or culturally *Western* association of music with magic and 'revelation'.[11] To begin with, the initially obscure character of Chowrimootoo's 'sentimental' might be set aside in favour of registering richer and perhaps more deeply troubling matters of feeling – of engagement with the mysteries and fragilities of life and of the world in which we find ourselves.

* * *

Let me begin by suggesting that, however we might characterize his music and those to whom it spoke during his lifetime, Britten himself seems to have been rarely anything other than inescapably 'highbrow'. Class played its part, in its complex English way. Humphrey Carpenter, in his first quasi-official biography of the composer in 1992, was inclined to support Britten's own claim to have come from "a very ordinary middle-class family."[12] Whatever the status of dentists, like his father, in early twentieth-century Lowestoft, the present writer – as the member of a decidedly lower-middle-class family of the 1950s – finds Carpenter's account of the composer's schooling and of the Brittens' home life, with its musical soirées and so on, suggestive of a decidedly upper-middle-class atmosphere, in behaviour and aspiration, if not necessarily of wealth. One might imagine it being as vulnerably posh as the composer's choice of texts recently struck a friend of mine – a highly intelligent painter, of unprivileged background, who had been a special-needs teaching assistant in a far-from-middle-class school with whose pupils he sought to empathize to clearly great effect. He professed himself to feel alienated from the literary taste of the *Serenade for Tenor, Horn and Strings*, to which I had enthusiastically attempted to introduce him. "I can't *stand* the Romantic poets" was his no doubt sub-middlebrow response, rather putting me in my place as the product of a lower-middle-class family whose aspirations to higher middle-class status had, in the end, been more or less successful. My father's efforts as a partly self-taught accountant even enabled him to finance my attendance at a private, fee-paying secondary school (I failed my '11-plus' examination) which facilitated my eventual path to becoming the first member of either his or my mother's family to go to university (albeit an uncloistered, 'new' university like York).

Yet highbrow and high class as Britten seemed (particularly when he spoke on the radio or in the occasional TV interviews in which I first heard his voice), there was something about his music that reached and 'touched' a wider audience than might otherwise have been expected of a composer of 'modern music' of the kind that distressed my uncle. By the late 1960s Britten had become a national celebrity of sorts, supported by royalty and loved by many lesser mortals to be found in the ranks of the aspiring middlebrow amongst whom I must surely number myself (from a Chowrimootian point of view). That was when I escaped suburbia for the mediaeval charm of York, with its ultra-modern new university campus outside the city walls. *Within* those walls, Mellers was steering his pioneering Music department towards The New, even as he generously and famously embraced everything from Beethoven to the Beatles (via Harry Partch and John Coltrane, along with Couperin, Bach and a great deal else).[13]

8 *The Roots of My Musical Taste and Chowrimootoo's Worry*

By then Britten was already in my blood, as it were, as an aspiring highbrow who had yet to recognize his inner middle-brow, as signified, no doubt, by my ready taste for, and readiness to respond to 'sentiment' – but was that with or without the supposedly sickly '-ality'? What follows is, indeed, an attempt to challenge the evaluative criteria underlying Chowrimootoo's erased but implied definition of what that sentimentality *is* which he seeks to repress within himself and whose presence in *Peter Grimes* he disparages on obscurely justified, medicalized grounds. This, we have seen, he even suggests was 'heard' by the period ear in the fifth, 'Moonlight' interlude. Call me old-fashioned, but as the possessor of a perhaps more nearly period ear than his (not that this grants me any right of veto or undue authority), I am bound to come clean and confess that I have always cherished it as a moving evocation of the pain of regret and loss that might conceivably trouble the lonely contemplation of a calm moonlit sea on a summer's night.

'Noye's Fludde' from the Pews

Compared with Heather Wiebe's subtle and richly contextualized treatment of Britten's *Noye's Fludde* in *Britten's Unquiet Pasts* or with Philip Rupprecht's intricately sensitive readings of it in *Britten's Musical Language*,[14] Chowrimootoo's references to the composer's 1958 reworking of one of the Chester Miracle Plays seem coloured by an occasionally resentful critical anger. Perhaps it is the inevitable obverse of the sentimentality of which he disapproves. He describes its opening "with timpani roaring and congregation bellowing," after having previously characterized the accompanying congregational hymn as "browbeating" – referencing W. Anthony Sheppard's comment on hymn singing as "one of the most coercive of musical gestures."[15] I am bound to write somewhat differently, and yes, somewhat sentimentally about that work, which afforded me my first significant immersion in Britten's musical world. Shortly before Christmas, in December 1960, my all-boys secondary school was mobilized by its energetic music master to stage a performance of *Noye's Fludde*, just two years after its Aldeburgh premiere.

As a fee-paying 'public school', it was in some sense a bastion of middle-class sensibilities and values: a day school that had originally been founded to cater for less wealthy local families, unable to afford to send their sons to an elite boarding school that was once not far away. With just over 400 pupils, our school was at that time a smallish repository of the 'would-be-but-just-missed'. Many, like myself, had failed their '11-plus' examination and would have been condemned to a local comprehensive school, but for their parents' determination to 'give them a decent education'. The school was staffed mostly by men who had served in the army during and just after the Second World War. A few were very good, others were caricatures of the philistine military types whom Owen Wingrave might have had to confront. Some of them frequently turned up in military battle-dress (khaki uniforms and shiny leather boots) on the days the school 'corps'[16] was due to exercise in the afternoon. Then our militarily inclined (and/or parentally persuaded) contemporaries, similarly uniformed, would be lined up in rows on the playground, while marginalized opt-out non-participants like myself and my friends were occupied with the 'theatre group', helping the art master construct and paint scenery and, in this instance, the *papier-mâché* animal masks for the school's production of *Noye's Fludde*.

It was in that way that I, an unprepossessing and rather unpromising member of the lower, 'B' stream, was first drawn into contact with Britten's music. I was about to turn 13 by the time the production took place in a local church. I wasn't even invited to perform in it (our teacher would have had no inkling of my ostensibly talent-less musical inclinations at that time), but I must have shown sufficient willing to have been put to use as a kind of usher in the church, leading parents and other audience members to available places in the pews and handing out programmes. It meant that I was proudly 'involved', and could be seen to be by my parents when they came to the performance. It also meant that I heard and saw it on more than one occasion (I am surely recalling rehearsals rather than multiple performances, which the church would hardly have been in a position to welcome).

What I heard and experienced on 6th of December 1960 was inevitably mediated by my having grown up in the middle-class Church of England tradition of my parents, for whom church-going had been an established part of their lives since their own respective childhoods in large, impecunious families in the Hornsey area of North London. My respective grandfathers had been a latterly out-of-work vellum binder on my father's side, and a porter at Kings Cross station on my mother's. It brought to *our* childhood (that of me and my sister) that involvement with 'the Church' that meant not dogma or 'belief' in any very committed or intellectually embraced sense, but rather the social participation in a mutually supportive community, the focus of whose shared experience were the Sunday gatherings in St John's Church in Wembley.

It was set rather picturesquely in a spacious churchyard with overhanging trees. For Sunday services we dressed up to sit in reverential silence, aspiring to solemnity, while observing the rituals of the vestment-draped vicar and his curate, with the all-male choir, boys at the front in their blue cassocks, white surplices and starched and pleated 'ruffs' (I was one of their number for some years). We kneeled for prayers, sat to listen to 'lessons' read from the Bible and stood, often with relief, to sing the hymns, some of which were poetically striking, others incomprehensible, just a series of words and syllables to fit to melodies of similarly varied quality (although the best could be glorious to sing). Coerced? Hardly, in mine or my mother's case – she loved to sing along in her light soprano voice. More so, perhaps, in my father's, who like many of the 'professional' men in the congregation, were happier marshalling others and collecting service books than giving voice in the hymns, which they did in a sort of embarrassed *mezza voce*. My father could never decide which octave he should be singing in and would shift awkwardly and unexpectedly from one to another, as the line either fell too low or climbed too high for comfort. Only a few brave or annoying, self-regarding 'pushy' types would venture to 'bellow'. The overall effect was more one of muted 'following along': a sort of staggered shadowing of the organist and choir with a mildly embarrassed, half-sung, half silently mouthed moaning sound, relished by the few, admittedly dreaded by others, but respected by all. The hymns' endings were certainly welcomed as a kind of liberation from embarrassing involvement with confessing (and in song!) to strange and wild sentiments with which we would have been unlikely to evince much sympathy outside the church. But one felt better for having been through it, often indeed uplifted. You suffered, sometimes enjoyed, the whole experience in order to relish all the more the eventual release into the rest of Sunday: the roast lunch, the walk, something on the telly. It would simply not have been the same if we hadn't submitted to the shared ritual, with its pleasures, its repressions and sometimes (as in Holy Communion, when the vicar was in charge) a carefully managed dramatic structure that built up to the telling of the Last Supper and the processing up the aisle to receive the 'body and blood of Christ' on our knees at the altar rail – and to experience? Well, something of a kind of mysterious benediction and significance that was all in the act: less demonstrative of a commitment to 'faith' in the spooky business of transubstantiation than a belief in the significance of the ritual and the symbolism of the shared drama.

I find myself recalling all this in order to evoke something of the complex way in which *Noye's Fludde* moved me, as embracing something at once familiar and startling, even a little shocking. Was so colourful, noisy and moving a drama, with brightly painted pieces of scenery and dancing animals, even quite proper in church? It was perhaps a sign of the nascent rebel within me that I eventually found it both comfortingly familiar and rather gloriously subversive. Comforting were the hymns. They were what I was used to hearing when participating in those Sunday church services; and the first was rather a good one: the familiar, slightly grudging (rather than 'coerced'?) *mezza voce* sound of the congregation typically drifting in slightly late and trailing behind the choir and (on this occasion) orchestra. But rather than "browbeating", those three initial and subsequently reiterated orchestral chords seemed excitingly alive by comparison with the audience/congregation cautiously singing of their inadequacies in the minor key and modest stepwise motion of the tune 'Southwell' – rather appropriately, to my mind, recreating the sound of innumerable damp winter Evensongs that I had suffered as a choirboy. Those introductory flourishes of the motley band of players, young and old, professionals and squeaky beginners (school kids of all shapes, sizes and abilities), exploded with the lively irreverence of comic-book sound effects: "Ker*rumpf* – Ker*rumpf* - Ker*RUMPF*!" These promised music-making of an unbridled kind, way beyond the piety of the conventional hymn. And then came the Voice of God, proclaiming his instructions to Noye from a gallery at the back of the Church, in the highly imitable tones of our Maths master – way more impressive and measured, in spite of his difficulty with the 'th' sound, than the rather perfunctory deity of Trevor Anthony in the Britten recording. Mr Dickinson's "*I – God* – whom *all* ver *world* haf *wrought*" really seemed to mean what he said with ponderously accented, rhythmical emphasis on 'all', 'world' and 'wrought'.

The church now became a performance space – but performance of a much less controlled and pious nature than that of the usual priestly rituals. First came Noah's sons, led by a naughty boy from my form, who happened to have a rather pure treble voice. Running up the aisle as Sem, with his jaunty "Father, I am a ready bowne," he was followed by the other two with their carpentry tools. They soon began the construction of the Ark from brightly coloured pieces of scenery that fitted cleverly together to make the upper part of a stylized three-dimensional vessel with nobly rising prow. Mrs Noah rebelled, in spite of a further interruption by the Voice of God. But then came the dance-like processional march of the animals that now stole the show with their cleverly moulded and painted animal-head 'masks' (the work of art teacher Mr Allan and his helpers). They were accompanied by sometimes slightly bungling boy buglers from the school 'corps' (I presumed) who added in brazenly anarchic fashion (and *constructively*, for once, as we arty, non-military types reckoned) to the noisy merriment as each group of animals breathlessly reiterated their "Kyrie, kyrie – kyrie elei*son*!"

Only after the comic interlude of Mrs Noah and her Gossips – from whom she is eventually forcibly removed by her sons and brought into the Ark, where the children/animals now crowded behind its protective bulwarks – only then did Noah symbolically close his little cabin window, effectively readying the Ark for the coming flood. The storm began, with wet and windy recorders trembling amidst the graphically depicted raindrops of the slung mugs hit with wooden spoons. These sound effects contribute to the rising chaos of the storm, which is also a passacaglia, whose mysteriously upward creeping theme holds together the various windy and whining efforts of both professional and unprofessional ('beginner') string players. Meanwhile little painted 'waves' manipulated by eager crouching boys bobbed around the Ark. It was, as I recall, my first close encounter with a big span of real musical drama, building thrillingly to the point where the Ark's passengers master their panic to give voice to the second hymn in nervously prayerful hope: "Eternal Father strong to save. . . . Oh hear us when we cry to thee/ For those in peril on the sea." When the audience joins in for the next two verses, it has become an irresistibly involved congregation of supplicating participants in the drama:

> Oh Sacred Spirit who did'st brood
> Upon the chaos dark and rude,
> Who bad'st its angry tumult cease,
> And gavest light and life and peace.

Coercion must surely have given way to emotionally charged participation, however unexpected by the normally dutiful and conforming suburban parents, who had come intending just to support their offspring and smile distantly at their no doubt mildly embarrassing efforts. Instead, all were caught up in the magic of the returned light and peaceful redemption, once the dance episodes of the released raven and then the dove had brought the reward of the returned olive branch. The exotically archaic, but then still relatively familiar, sound of handbells now haloed the Voice of God with otherworldly clusters, eventually joining the more earthy celebration of the B-flat bugles that had accompanied the relieved Alleluias of the animals and their human companions. God benignly declared the storm over (fearful though the dissonant outburst of the organ that usually stands in for him in church), permitting the arrival of the painted sun, moon and stars along with an arching rainbow fixed to proudly raised broom handles. Rupprecht writes wonderfully about the "tingling interplay of separate tonal claims (with the F-naturals of the bell clusters rubbing up against the F-sharps in the hymn tune)."[17] At the time the effect was more truly transfiguring than anything I had experienced in the more discreet dramas of Sunday services. The final hymn may well have encouraged something closer to 'bellowing' – a fuller sound, less repressed perhaps, for Tallis's wonderfully 'grounded' canon sung to Addison's arcane and antiquated words of 'enlightened' faith – words that might have stuck perplexingly in the memory not only of their sons and daughters on stage but also of the mothers in their tidy kitchens and fathers on their commuter trains the next day:

> What though in solemn silence all
> Move round the dark terrestrial ball;
> What though nor real voice nor sound
> Amid their radiant orbs be found.
>
> In reason's ear they all rejoice
> And utter forth a glorious voice,
> For ever singing as they shine
> 'The hand that made us is Divine.'

"Did we really sing that?" they might have wondered. "What *does* it mean? Poetry? Well it was certainly something." I for one was hooked.[18]

Notes

1 This view of Vaughan Williams was emphasized in war-time radio talks by Hubert Foss. See Duncan Hinnells, *An Extraordinary Performance. Hubert Foss, Music, and the Oxford University Press* (Oxford and New York: Oxford University Oress, 1998), 35–6.

2 See Alain Frogley, 'Vaughan Williams and Nazi Germany: the 1937 Hamburg Shakespeare Prize' in Christa Brüstle and Guido Heldt (eds.), *Music as a Bridge. Musikalische Beziehungen zwischen England und Deutschland 1920–1950* (Hildesheim, Zürich and New York: Georg Olms Verlag, 2005), 113–32.
3 Heather Wiebe, *Britten's Unquiet Pasts. Sound and Memory in Postwar Reconstruction* (Cambridge: Cambridge University Press, 2012/15), 1.
4 See Foreword, Note 1.
5 Chowrimootoo, *Middlebrow Modernism*, ix.
6 Ibid., 56.
7 Respectively drawn from material quoted in Humphrey Carpenter, *Benjamin Britten. A Biography* (London: Faber and Faber, 1992), 69 and 300.
8 See Susan McClary, 'Terminal Prestige the Case of Avant-Garde Music Composition' in David Schwarz, Anahid Kassabian and Lawrence Siegel (eds.), *Keeping Score. Music, Disciplinarity, Culture* (Charlottesville and London: University Press of Virginia, 1997), 54–74. The essay first appeared in 1988.
9 Dai Griffiths, 'On Grammar Schoolboy Music' in Derek B. Scott (ed.), *Music, Culture & Society, A Reader* (Oxford: Oxford University Press, 2000/2002), 143–5. I return to the specific musicological agenda of 'middlebrow' studies below in *Secondary School Britten; 'The Turn of the Screw* see p. 17ff.
10 In 1974, the success of Dr Jacob Bronowki's 1973 TV series *The Ascent of Man* brought the scientist onto Parkinson's show to face the final question "Should we take note of anything you say?" His response included the phrase quoted.
11 See Wilfrid Mellers, *Caliban Reborn. Renewal in Twentieth-Century Music* (London: Victor Gollancz Ltd., 1968). Mellers' first chapter is titled 'Revelation and Incarnation. The Legacy of the Past'; the last reverses the formula as 'Incarnation and Revelation: The Promise of the Future; a Theme in Stravinsky, Britten and Maxwell Davies'. With the concept of 'incarnation' Mellers alluded to the Christian notion of a numinous deity 'becoming man': we may bear *within ourselves* the inheritance of a 'spirit' which we desire to 'express' rather than to evoke or conjure by means of forgetting, or transcending the embodied 'self'. A modest, ideologically revealing, version of such 'revelatory' music is requested by Sir Thomas Bertram in Jane Austen's novel *Mansfield Park*. Having returned to disrupt and prevent the theatrical entertainment his family had been preparing in his absence, he bids his daughters to provide some evening music, which "helped to conceal the want of real harmony" in the family unit (*Mansfield Park*, Book Two, Ch. 2).
12 See Carpenter, *Benjamin Britten*, 4.
13 In 1966 the York Music Department was still accommodated in two houses in Micklegate, in the heart of the mediaeval city, into which we travelled daily by bus (we lived on the new campus at Heslington).
14 Wiebe, *Britten's Unquiet Pasts*, Chapter 5, 'Remembering faith in *Noye's Fludde*', 151–90; Philip Rupprecht, *Britten's Musical Language* (Cambridge: Cambridge University Press, 2001), 21–9.

14 *The Roots of My Musical Taste and Chowrimootoo's Worry*

15 See Chowrimootoo, *Middlebrow Modernism*, 123–4 and 205, Note 40.
16 Pronounced 'core', in the French manner, these military bodies within schools of a certain kind were often referred to as 'OTCs', meaning Officer Training Corps, designed to prepare voluntary participants for higher-level entry into the armed services.
17 Rupprecht, *Britten's Musical Language*, 25. Rupprecht continues" "The higher brightenesses of the bell overtones correspond to the rainbow itself appearing on stage as God speaks. Addison's hymn meanwhile forms the sounding earthbound contemplation of 'the spacious firmament' in which the rainbow shines." Ibid., 25–7.
18 Credit here to Paul Kildea for referencing Wes Anderson's wonderful 2012 film *Moonrise Kingdom*, which quirkily records something of the effect *Noyes Fludde* and *The Young Person's Guide to the Orchestra* had on impressionable twelve-year-olds of those times (here on an island off the coast of New England in 1965). See Paul Kildea, *Benjamin Britten. A Life in the Twentieth Century* (London: Penguin Books, 2014), 37 [note]. [Kildea's biography was initially published by Allen Lane in 2013].

2 Secondary-School Britten: *The Turn of the Screw*

However I might try to evoke the immediacy of my first experience of *Noye's Fludde*, my retrospective understanding of it is inevitably coloured by Wilfrid Mellers's treatment of it in his 1968 book *Caliban Reborn: Renewal in Twentieth-Century Music*, published during my second year as one of his students at York. Just as that book's title avoided partitioning Twentieth-Century Music by brow, modernity or whatever, so the whole dizzying range of his examples of musical 'renewal' seems to celebrate in ecumenical embrace works of the many composers who moved and interested him. These ranged from Wagner (*Tristan*) through Debussy to Boulez, Cage and the Beatles. Bob Dylan, Schoenberg and Webern also have walk-on parts. Interestingly, Berg did not figure, although his *Wozzeck* became the well-worn stick with which self-styled 'highbrows' would beat *Peter Grimes*. Without any apology, Mellers introduces *Noye's Fludde* there as a work of Britten's that "should deserve to be rated among his supreme achievements." He went on to justify his suggestion in seven pages of intensely engaged sympathetic analysis that were understandably reprinted as a stand-alone essay in Christopher Palmer's *The Britten Companion* in 1984.[1] In that volume it follows another Mellers essay on an earlier, very different work, to which my curious musical fate led me for what would become my third close encounter with Britten's music.

Before that, the enterprising teacher who had been responsible for our school production of *Noye's Fludde* arranged as a kind of sequel in the following November what would prove my second close encounter. By some means or other, my musical enthusiasm had now communicated itself sufficiently that it was as a more-than-willing member of the school choir that I took part in the performance of Britten's cantata *St Nicolas* in a venerable hall, not far from the church where *Noye's Fludde* had been performed. The concert involved large forces that included the choir of a nearby grammar school for girls and our teacher's own adult group called the Sine Nomine Singers; Wilfred Brown was the tenor. *St Nicolas* was performed in the first half, after which a William Boyce Symphony and Vaughan Williams's *Concerto Grosso for String Orchestra* flanked a performance by the Sine Nomine Singers of Britten's *Rejoice in the Lamb*, during which I presume we would

16   *Secondary-School Britten:* The Turn of the Screw

have remained in our seats as spectators. I am ashamed to have no recollection of the concert after *St Nicolas*; I had much enjoyed the way its dramatic narrative of the saint's life unfolded, from the merry business of the dance-like chorus "Nicolas was born in answer to prayer" – in which the boy's voice calling out "God be glorified" is later transformed into that of the adult tenor – to the deliciously gruesome tale of the pickled boys. And once again there were the congregational hymns ('All people that on earth do dwell' and 'God moves in a mysterious way') in which, as would have been unproblematically expected in those days, our parents in the audience joined in when our teacher turned to 'conduct' them. The programme had announced that "the next concert" would include Stravinsky's *Symphony of Psalms* and Britten's *Missa Brevis* – boldly, as it now seems, setting the two great living modern composers side by side.

It was consequently something of a shock when that same teacher suddenly announced his departure from the school at the end of my third year, in the summer of 1962. On the verge of making my choice of which 'O-level' subjects to concentrate on for the next two years, firmly intending to choose Music as one of them, I was devastated. In his place there now arrived an even younger, new Cambridge graduate (just six years older than us) whom we came to know just by his first name. I will call him Harry – it was a mark of respect that he acquired no satirical nickname. A singer and actor with little conducting experience, he bravely took over direction of the performance of Stravinsky's *Symphony of Psalms* that had already been set in motion, scheduled for Saturday, 3rd November 1962. By that time, as an official O-level Music student, I was inevitably involved again as a singer in the choir for the Stravinsky, which newly arrived Harry conducted in the first part of a programme from whose second half the difficult Britten *Missa Brevis* had been removed. It still comprised two orchestral works: a new *Passacaglia for Brass and Percussion* by a local composer and Handel's *Music for the Royal Fireworks*. Between those, our former teacher returned with his Sine Nomine Singers to offer a performance of Britten's *Ode to St Cecilia*, of which I similarly, and sadly, have no recollection, although I was later to get to know it well. Once again, I suspect that we would have been kept in place to listen to the last part of the concert.

What I definitely do remember was the very first live opera that I ever saw, just a few days later. By November 1962, not least with that memorable performance of the Stravinsky, Harry had won us over as one of the most charismatic and energetic directors of Music that any school could have hoped for. Our small group of O-level Music candidates studied their set works with him (these included Handel's *Semele*, the César Franck Symphony in D minor, Tchaikovsky's Fantasy Overture *Romeo and Juliet* and Mozart's Symphony no. 39). They certainly did not include the modern opera we attended at Sadler's Wells that autumn. The series 'Your Opera Nights' was part of Sir Robert Mayer's 'Youth and Music' scheme, in which Harry had wisely enrolled the school. He encouraged us to attend many of its events with him. He certainly prepared us well for the opera to be performed on 7th November 1962, spending more or less an entire lesson telling us the story – in memorably captivating fashion – of *The Turn of the Screw*.

What a remarkable and bold choice it was. A short piece by Sir Robert Mayer, headed 'Bright Future', was included in the flimsy little eight-page programme book, whose listing of the ten vice presidents of Youth and Music included 'Mr Benjamin Britten' along with Sir John Barbirolli, Mr Yehudi Menuhin and Sir Malcolm Sargent. Mayer identified the roots of his organization in the French 'Jeunesse Musicales' movement started during the Second World War "for the purpose of attracting to music an older age-group." He went on to explain that

> Youth and Music was, however, even more concerned with the position at home and, as a result of hard work, is now able to offer exceptional opportunities in the spheres of opera, concerts and lectures to its members: people up to approximately 25 years in all walks of life.

This might have recommended itself to Christopher Chowrimootoo as evidence of the broadly 'middlebrow' nature of the Youth and Music project, along the lines of individuals and organizations in America devoted to popularizing literature and the arts.

These represent the primary subject matter of Joan Shelley Rubin's 1992 study *The Making of Middlebrow Culture*, which has been influential on the Middlebrow Studies movement in musicology. This has sought to explore the historical category of middlebrow as involving the popularization and dissemination of consumably 'high' cultural values to those seeking aspirationally to avoid the class-bound stigma of 'lowbrow' taste.[2] Chowrimootoo's chapter on *The Turn of the Screw* is, however, rather revealingly occupied with an implied high modernist critique of the horror genre and "Gothic Melodrama"[3] as reflected in the "crude and melodramatic literalism" of *The Turn of the Screw*.[4] This description seems to highlight a conflict arising from his evident grasp of high modernist hang-ups about such things in those times. He frequently airs some of them, as when he appears to accuse modernist critics of over-obsessing about what he calls the opera's merely opportunistic use of "note rows" and related formal principles while overlooking its "Gothic" aspects, which could (presumably?) have let them off the analytical hook to criticize the work more securely on grounds of its evidently distasteful popularism – and this at the same time as hinting (fairly enough) that many other iconic works of modernism were using those same 'advanced' techniques and predominantly dissonant harmonic textures to create disturbing psychological melodramas borne of 'sentimental' overload (think of *Erwartung*? think of *Wozzeck*?). Such things, he suggests, had been the stuff of much nineteenth-century opera and the literature on which it drew, emblematically including Shakespeare's Lady Macbeth and the Ghost of Hamlet's father.

18 *Secondary-School Britten:* The Turn of the Screw

While 'middlebrow' scholarship frequently ends up begging questions about the nature of the compromisingly *highbrow* perspective on which its categorization mostly relies, my 15-year-old self was innocent of any knowledge of such matters, given my ignorance both of the formal derivation of its thematic material or of the opera's structural organization as a Theme with sixteen variations that make up the eight scenes of each act (the Prologue leading to the presentation of the Theme). The possibility that Britten might in some sense even have been gently thumbing his nose at the musical modernists here seems to have occurred as little to Chowrimootoo in 2018 as it did to me in 1962. In the former's complicatedly ambivalent chapter on the opera, he appears, as always, to use the carefully researched and recovered views of contemporary critics to support his own reading of the opera as "failing to reconcile" the aesthetic opposites of "modernist psychodrama and Gothic melodrama," for all that he accepts that Britten may have revealed "the unsettling commonalities between the two traditions."⁵ But unsettling to *whom*? – we may ask. It is difficult to avoid the suspicion that they are unsettling to Chowrimootoo by virtue of their threatening to penetrate his austere "modernist exterior" with sickly sentimentality. As a 15-year-old devotee of Sunday afternoon Hollywood melodramas from the 1930s and '40s on TV, *The Turn of the Screw* proved for me a rather easily grasped 'first opera', which unwittingly provided access to an older form of musically enhanced melodrama derived from the long tradition of such things – whether in the theatre, in the cinema or in literature. Staged 'melodramas' had been as popular in appeal as they were often complex in psychological implication for a good half century or more. In the 1860s, Queen Victoria and her beloved Albert were admiring consumers of the increasingly technologically elaborate stagecraft of such theatre. Once the genre had crossed the river in London from the disreputable south side to the more elegant north, its productions became harbingers of an ever more inclusive form of theatrical entertainment.⁶ This was one in which intellectual complexity and visceral thrills were drawn together by technological modernity into an influential testing ground for the mass-entertainment cinema that would soon appropriate (and thus effectively supersede) its manners and mechanics.

The unsigned 'Programme Note' in the meagre little booklet that I carefully preserved as a memento of that first opera visit emphasized the 'conflict' in the story between desired innocence and the feared subversions of 'abnormality'. Having set out the characters and the dramatic situation in its first paragraph, crediting Henry James's original story, the note stressed that the governess's initial "happy impressions of the house and the children" are soon shattered by the appearance of the ghost of Peter Quint:

> Later it becomes clear that the children are aware of the ghosts but are deliberately concealing their knowledge from their elders.

Sadler's Wells Trust Ltd.
Director Norman Tucker
Administrative Director Stephen Arlen
presents

Sadler's Wells Opera

Musical Director Colin Davis
Director of Productions Glen Byam Shaw

Sadler's Wells presents in association with The Royal Opera House, Covent Garden, the English Opera Group production of

The Turn of the Screw
by Benjamin Britten

Libretto, after Henry James' story, by Myfanwy Piper

Scenery and costumes designed by John Piper

Conductor Meredith Davies

Producer Basil Coleman

Wednesday 7 November 1962
9th Performance at Sadler's Wells

First performance by the English Opera Group, Teatro la Fenice, Venice, 14 September 1954. First performance in this country, Sadler's Wells Theatre, 6 October 1954, again by the English Opera Group.

Sadler's Wells Theatre was re-opened by Lilian Baylis on 6 January 1931

Sadler's Wells Trust Ltd. works in full association with the Arts Council of Great Britain

The Turn of the Screw

The Prologue..................John Lanigan
The Governess.................Jennifer Vyvyan
Miles ⎫ children in her charge ⎧ David Pinto
Flora ⎭   ⎩ Ellen Dales
Mrs. Grose, the housekeeper...........Sylvia Fisher
Quint, a former manservant...........John Lanigan
Miss Jessel, a former governess........Elizabeth Fretwell

The Prologue

Act 1.   Scene 1 — The Journey
         Scene 2 — The Welcome
         Scene 3 — The Letter
         Scene 4 — The Tower
         Scene 5 — The Window
         Scene 6 — The Lesson
         Scene 7 — The Lake
         Scene 8 — At Night

Act II   Scene 1 — Colloquy and Soliloquy
         Scene 2 — The Bells
         Scene 3 — Miss Jessel
         Scene 4 — The Bedroom
         Scene 5 — Quint
         Scene 6 — The Piano
         Scene 7 — Flora
         Scene 8 — Miles

At the Lyceum Theatre, Sheffield tonight Sadler's Wells Opera is performing "The Bartered Bride"

Figure 2.1 The two central pages of the Sadler's Wells programme for *The Turn of the Screw* on 7th November 1962.

Source: (Author's collection)

20 *Secondary-School Britten:* The Turn of the Screw

I recall finding it easy to grasp that the supposedly innocent normality sought or imagined by the governess and Mrs Grose was threatened by the deeper and more complex 'knowingness' of the children. The Gothic, melodramatic aspect of the whole thing I took easily in my stride, as a result of which I may then, as later, have found the quoted, but musically 'manipulated', nursery rhymes complicatedly more spooky and unsettling (and more appropriate to much younger children?) than the sight of Quint behind the big, gauze-covered window that appears in one of Chowrimootoo's illustrations of the original 1954 staging. That must clearly have been what I was privileged to see revived in 1962. The programme certainly attributed scenery and costumes to John Piper and the production to Basil Coleman. The performance I saw even included the original Governess (Jennifer Vyvyan).

Piper's big Gothic window was significant in that one of my friends who attended that evening had heard Harry's detailed explanation of the plot but, being no less of a novice opera-goer than I, had assured us that if the ghost appeared at a window and started *singing*, he would have hysterics. We laughed at the suggestion (I uneasily, suspecting that this would inevitably happen, as it did). But there was no laughter in the theatre that night; we were all thoroughly gripped by the drama, which seemed to defuse the unfamiliarity and ostensible oddity of this form of musical theatre.

And theatre it certainly was. I recall the visual (and musical) effect of the cleverly simulated final stage of the governess's journey in the small carriage in which she arrives at Bly and the way lighting was used to create quick, filmic changes of scene. I also remember the visual effect of the colloquy between John Lanigan (as Quint) and Elizabeth Fretwell (as Miss Jessel) which took place behind a full 'gauze' – a magical stage effect, now rarely seen, with which I was familiar from some of the big London pantomimes we had been taken to as children. I feel sure that I was touched by the powerful musical effect of their climactic declamation of the then-mysterious Yeats line: "The ceremony of innocence is drowned." I certainly recall being impressed by the shivery melismas of Quint's calling of Miles's name in Scene 8 (with hair-raising, ghostly tinkling from the celesta) – no less by Miles's little 'Malo' song and by the desperation of the governess's tragic recollection of it at the end, after Miles's terrifying, angry bridging of the worlds of imagination and reality when he sings no more but finally shouts out "Peter Quint, you devil!" before dying in her arms. It had been a memorably un-alienating if excitingly scary introduction to the world of opera. And I probably grasped more of the dark secret of Quint's devilry than I should, to judge from later readings of the work by Philip Brett and Harper-Scott. It certainly prepared me well to agree with Chowrimootoo's striking comment that "in its notorious attempt to shock and unsettle audiences, one might even describe modernism as the epitome of Gothic melodrama."[7] There, surely, Britten was right on the money.

Music A-level and 'War Requiem'

More opera trips followed, and Sadlers Wells became a familiar haunt – the theatre where *The Turn of the Screw* had received its first British staging (after the Venice premiere) and where *Peter Grimes* had first been performed. A band of us eagerly followed Harry's lead as he sought to broaden our musical-dramatic horizons. One of our O-level set works was Handel's rarely performed *Semele*, in relation to which he took us up to see *Xerxes* in June 1963, so that we could get a sense of Handelian opera on the stage (for all that *Semele* was pragmatically characterized as an 'oratorio'). The following year we went up to see *Cosi fan Tutte*. By 1965 I was a Sixth Form A-level student and going for all that was on offer.

During that period, I had moved on from our little O-level group to being the sole person in my year to opt for A-level Music – studying on my own with Harry rather successfully for two years, during which he variously guided, criticized or celebrated my efforts as appropriate, respectively to my harmony and counterpoint and to the quality of my essay-writing. The former I found a struggle, but we managed. He had laughed heartily and rather mercilessly at the O-level essay I had written on Tchaikovsky's *Romeo and Juliet* overture, where I had quoted the composer supposedly worrying about his formal grasp and the fact that "his seams showed" (only later did I get the joke), but our relationship over the advanced-level set works became almost collegial. Harry was happiest with the vocal and operatic ones, whereas I could lead somewhat on orchestral music, being by that time steeped in Tchaikovsky and a whole range of works, including symphonies and concertos whose scores I had begun to collect and that I was fortunate to be able to access in popular concerts (including the Proms) and 'Tchaikovsky evenings' at the Royal Albert Hall. Whenever they were available, I would choose the 'choir' seats, usually behind the percussion; they cost just 11/6 a time – 65p in the decimal currency to come. The sense of being almost part of the orchestra made up for the skewed sound effect in that hall where some of the expensive stalls seats were much worse, before the famous acoustic 'mushrooms' were suspended from the ceiling.

I can never thank the Oxford and Cambridge Examination Board of that era enough for the A-level set works they chose for me. In a sense they made me what I was to become. There was an opera, Verdi's *Rigoletto*, and there was a Mahler symphony, mercifully the First – although when I appeared at the bookshop to collect my ordered score, I insisted that it must be wrong as the grey/blue Universal Edition study score was so much larger than the yellow Eulenburg miniatures I was used to. The charming little lady who served us assured me that it was right – and I soon came to treasure it. As if that was not enough to get to grips with, we had also to tackle the Ravel 'Introduction and Allegro' (which I also grew to love) and, rather anomalously, the Palestrina *Pope Marcellus Mass*. Even that was not all. There was one more mighty work to set alongside the Verdi and the Mahler: the Britten *War Requiem*, just three years after its premiere. I remembered our former teacher insisting that we make the effort to listen to it on the radio back in May 1962. I *think* I did, although I sadly cannot recall any impression of what I heard. I evidently wrote in to the BBC to obtain a copy of the text, which they published in 1963 for the modest price of one shilling – something they occasionally, and rather wonderfully, would do at that time with new works or the libretti of unfamiliar operas.[8]

* * *

Chowrimootoo's research into contemporary criticism can be relied upon to have missed few of the carefully crafted put-downs from the period. Stravinsky was expert at these, not least where Britten was concerned:

> Stravinsky [. . .] insisted that the adulatory reception accorded the *War Requiem* 'was a phenomenon as remarkable as the music itself.'
> Although Stravinsky emphasized the critical creativity involved in sublimating Britten's works, he also implied that the music – with its fake counterpoint, cinematic grandeur and counterfeit modernism – invited the press dissimilation [sic] it eventually received.[9]

Mervyn Cooke has nevertheless drawn attention to the fact that Stravinsky's comments "have often been selectively quoted to give the impression that he was critical of Britten's *music*. In fact, his comments were strictly confined to discussing . . . the 'hype' surrounding the early performances of the *War Requiem*."[10] Happily, the now all too innocent-seeming reverence and awe generated by studying the *War Requiem* in 1965–6 was untroubled by anything beyond the growing admiration that Harry and I shared for it. Gradually we came to terms with how it worked and was structured – no less with what it was trying to achieve and the powerful impact it had upon us, as it had upon its first audience.

With the benefit of hindsight, I can understand the critical thrust of Stravinsky's desire to retain and guard a kind of modernist high ground in the face of Britten's widely appreciated contribution to the celebration of the consecration of Basil Spence's new Coventry Cathedral (the old one having been bombed to a shell during the Second World War). However unintentionally, it perhaps challenged Stravinsky to question whether 'his' territory, whose desecration he felt the *War Requiem* and its reception represented, might comparatively have been an obscure, if exotic, valley garden. Joke-mongering aside, I am bound to ask what Chowrimootoo's own selective quotations of Stravinsky on Britten were really trying to achieve. By digging evidence of the "adulatory reception" of the *War Requiem* out of the artificial flower beds of nefarious *critics* (no middlebrow scholar will apparently waste time on the benighted representatives of the paying masses who queued to get into the cathedral to

Secondary-School Britten: The Turn of the Screw 23

hear it), he is clearly defending his own "austere modernist" patio on which nothing inspiring "sentimental" admiration is permitted to grow. We might, nevertheless, be justified in asking more soberly what that verb 'sublimating' is really doing in this context, and what he means by 'fake counterpoint' (is not *all* counterpoint in Western music in some sense 'faked'? – manufactured in accordance with established rules?).

Of course, Chowrimootoo's primary concern is with the operas, and I can only respond to his tendentious use of Stravinsky's bitter-seeming mockery of *War Requiem* by re-evoking the memory of opening that score, and the similarly shiny black box of the famously high-selling recording of 1963, with its (yes) deliberately austere, white-lettered title, and placing the first disc on the old-style turntable. I am still fired by the desire to seek ever better words with which to describe what I found myself confronting. First the extraordinary *dramatic* counterpoint of the opening section: the solemnly unfolding recitative of the orchestral strings, over pedal 'A's and with a key signature indicating D minor (there is even some real counterpoint going on in the accompanying woodwind). It could almost be the long-unfolding subject of a Bartokian fugue. I came later to wonder if it might allude to the opening of Mahler's posthumous Tenth Symphony. We then pause for the ritualistically reiterated words from the Latin 'Mass for the Dead' on F-sharp, "Requiem, requiem aeternam" ('Rest eternal [grant them Lord]'). Sopranos and tenors seem to be closely following each other, as in priestly/congregational responses. The string line resumes, and the next interruption by the choir is by altos and basses, with the same words, but on C, setting up the devilish tritone that we might not expect to have encountered in or near the chancel of a newly consecrated cathedral.[11]

What I am calling the 'dramatic counterpoint' here soon acquires a further layer as distant boys voices enter with a more conventional hymn ("Songs of praise are due to Thee, God in Zion"/ *Te decet hymnus*. . .). Their assured, faster-paced jauntiness suggests the uncritical rehearsal of conventional faith – the boys' distant placement enhances their impersonal, decidedly unsentimental assurance until those final words ("hear my prayer, all flesh shall come to Thee."). These fade on repeated notes, a tritone apart, that bring us back to the darker, far less self-assured lamentation of the main choir as its "Requiem aeternam" returns at Cue 7, developing rather as before until it dies away, with the last "dona eis Domine," on lines once more a tritone apart. This contemplative solemnity is itself then broken into by the chamber orchestra accompanying the two male soloists: originally the British Peter Pears and the German Dietrich Fischer-Dieskau. The opening lines of this first of the interspersed settings of First World War poems by Wilfred Owen are accompanied by an uncaringly bouncy march in the strings and strange, whistling and whining sound effects from the flute and clarinet. They ask a darkly ironic question of the Requiem's formal, communally endorsed ritual of supplication, supported by ancestral 'faith'. As in *Noye's Fludde*, the Cathedral becomes a kind of theatre in which two individual participants in the war now ask, "What passing bells for those who die as cattle? Only the monstrous anger of the guns . . ." Poignantly, the possibility of some kind of dialogue between the separate layers of musical voicing is embraced at their reply to their own question ("What candles may be held to speed them all?") when they adopt the melody of the boys' previously faraway "Te decet hymnus" to propose, "Not in the hands of boys, but in their eyes/ Shall shine the holy glimmer of goodbyes./ The pallor of girls' brows shall be their pall."

But is that austere modernist realism, or some form of sickly sentimentality? The work itself encompasses the invitation to question each possibility, and responds to each in its way as the complex discourse established between the various layers of ritual and enactment, consolation and despair, plays out in the unfolding drama of the Requiem itself. The fundamental structure we know well enough from Verdi's and the many other settings of this venerable liturgical text. We know it must evoke the apocalyptically prophesied "Day of anger" [*Dies Irae*] – here with stunning effects of approaching military threat (fanfares and competing horn and trumpet signals). The angry threat must be realized, must "dissolve this generation into ashes" before the formal supplication of the *Offertorium*, whose reference to "Abraham and his offspring" inspires Britten's insertion of a setting of Owen's bitter poem 'The Parable of the Old Man and the Young'. Its music draws upon the composer's 1952 Canticle II ('Abraham and Isaac'); here Abraham pays no heed to God's eventual demand that he should spare the boy and "offer the ram of pride" instead:

> But the old man would not so, but slew his son, -
> And half the seed of Europe, one by one.

The dramatic shock keeps us preoccupied, at an awed distance from the magnificently brazen, exoticized *Sanctus*, with its 'oriental' bells and crescendo of muttered voices speaking "pleni sunt coeli." There follows the stunning simplicity of the *Agnus Dei*, where Owen's poem "One ever hangs where shelled roads part" takes centre-stage, relegating the chorus's singing of the Latin text to the role of chastened accompaniment. The perilously rising line of the solo tenor's appropriation of the closing "Dona nobis pacem" ("Grant us Thy peace") seems, however, to impress the main chorus to the extent that they now become active seekers after redemption in the *Libera me*. Their voices writhe in chromatic wailing from the depths of a despair that is finally confronted in explicit recollection of the *Dies Irae*, leading to the fearful climax at Cue 116, when their cries seem to seek liberation from the blindly marching melody of the initial Owen setting. Instead, a vastly slowed-down version of it becomes a dirge for all humanity. And then the final Owen setting: 'Strange Meeting', in which the two soldiers confront each other after death ("I am the enemy you killed, my friend"). At the close it inspires the full forces of both choirs to join in *its* final words: "Let us sleep now" – not (I would argue) 'sentimentally', but in an outpouring of sympathy and love that is finally capped by the cautious recapitulation of the mysterious cadential epilogue from the opening *Requiem aeternam*. Its 'Amen' achieves its tentative embrace of F major in sombre, hushed humility.

* * *

Quite what, as an eighteen-year-old, I managed to write about my 'set works' in the A-level examination, I do not recall; my score of the *War Requiem* gained copied-out quotations only from John Culshaw's notes to the Decca recording. It was, after all, too early for considered scholarly accounts of the work to have appeared in available writing about Britten. The Mahler literature in English was not significantly much better (at least as regards the contents of our school library). But we had the scores and we had recordings, and I would defend to the last our having been set those three big works (*Rigoletto*, Mahler's First Symphony and *War Requiem*). They were just what I needed to get my ears and mind working on at that age. My memory of studying them and gradually mapping for myself their structure and intention, in relation to what I could find out about the history of their respective genres, is one of intense absorption, richly rewarded. In the case of the Britten, it surely helped that Harry, as a singer, had come into contact with Philip Ledger at Cambridge, along with others who were linked in some way to the Aldeburgh 'set' about which so much has been written. He frequently commented on recent Britten works, like *A Midsummer Night's Dream*, and on Peter Pears's continuing work with Britten – albeit never venturing fully to address the nature of their relationship, since he knew that we all, as it were, 'knew'; he was also careful to remain inexplicit about his own sexuality in those days before decriminalization. The open secret was one which he and I privately shared in our own ways, having neither the language nor yet models for how such things might be dealt with, or even considered relevant, in the study of music.

It was all immensely and urgently exciting. Whatever I did, in the end, manage to write in my A-level examinations was sufficient to get me good passes both in Music and in English. For French I gained only a scraped Pass. But I managed to secure my place at York, for all that the school had a tradition of sending boys on to Cambridge. Harry had thoughtfully recommended that I consider Wilfrid Mellers's new department at York, feeling that I "was not ready for Oxbridge." At the time that estimation hurt slightly, even as I could sense how true it surely was. It was in a state of apprehensive uncertainty that I duly prepared to become the first member of my immediate family to go to university, heading off on the train to York in the autumn of 1966. There my experiences of Britten were to multiply, even as what I might call my 'inner compass' continued to point firmly towards Mahler and Vienna. Britten's own admiration for Mahler was at that time unknown to me.

Notes

1. Wilfrid Mellers, *Caliban Reborn. Renewal in Twentieth-Century Music*, 164 and Wilfrid Mellers, 'Through *Noyes Fludde*' in Christopher Palmer (ed.), *The Britten Companion* (London: Faber & Faber, 1984), 153–60.
2. Joan Shelley Rubin, *The Making of Middlebrow Culture* (Chapel Hill and London: The University of North Carolina Press, 1992). More will be found in the 2020 'Colloquy: Musicology and the Middlebrow' in *The Journal of the American Musicological Society*, Vol. 73, 2, 327–95. I return to this in Essay I **[III, 12]**.
3. Chowrimootoo, *Middlebrow Modernism*, 106.
4. Ibid., 112.
5. Ibid., 116.
6. See Michael V. Pisani, *Music for the Melodramatic Theatre in Nineteenth-Century London & New York* (Iowa City: University of Iowa Press, 2014), 186.
7. Chowrimootoo, *Middlebrow Modernism*, 115.
8. I still have that text, printed on rather stiff cream-coloured paper, with the title and the Wilfred Owen epigraph on the front cover of two folded sheets, making a booklet of 8 sides, the first two of which carried a Programme Note by Alec Robertson.
9. Chowrimootoo, *Middlebrow Modernism*, 21.
10. Mervyn Cooke, *Britten. 'War Requiem'*, Cambridge Music Handbooks (Cambridge: Cambridge University Press, 1996), 84. The matter of Stravinsky's thoughts about the *War Requiem* is also treated in Richard Taruskin, *Music in the Late Twentieth Century*, Vol. 5 of the *Oxford History of Western Music* (Oxford: Oxford University Press, 2010), 257–61.
11. Mediaeval superstition regarded the tense dissonance of this three wholetone interval as 'diabolus in musica', the devil in music.

3 Encountering Britten as a Music Student at York in the Late 1960s

If it was as a nervous 1960s Mahlerian that I arrived at the University of York for my first undergraduate year, I was also already one of 'Britten's children'.[1] My route into music had led me into a cultural landscape he had richly influenced. It was not, however, something I pondered very seriously at that time; there were too many other things to think about. I was initially enrolled on the Music and Education degree course, the Music part of which entailed having lectures on mediaeval music on Monday mornings and 'Twentieth-Century Music' on Friday mornings (both with Robert Sherlaw Johnson). In between, there were the more vexing Harmony and Counterpoint tutorials to produce work for, while reading novels by D. H. Lawrence and Raymond Williams and poetry by William Blake for the 'Education' part of the course. That I would drop by the end of the first year, becoming what was charmingly called a 'pure music' student – although its purity might in my case have been questioned with some justification.

Nevertheless, it was during that busy first year that I had two of my most significant, and quite unexpected, encounters with Britten. I remember them, for some reason, in reverse order, although I have before me the evidence of a cherished programme to confirm that in April 1967 I was encouraged by a fellow student (who probably considered himself a more committed 'English music' devotee than me) to join him in a trip to London to see a production of *Peter Grimes*. This would have been in the Easter vacation, so the logistics were relatively uncomplicated (my parents lived in London and my friend's in Chelmsford). What was special about that opera trip was that it was to the opening night of a revival of *Peter Grimes*, two years before the famous BBC film version of 1969 (I had of course watched the BBC's pioneering broadcast of *Billy Budd* in December 1966). The *Grimes* revival was in the same Sadler's Wells theatre as my first encounter with *The Turn of the Screw* – also, of course, on the very stage on which *Grimes* had been premiered in 1945, marking the theatre's re-opening after the war. Pears was once more appearing in the title role.

Of the other singers, I now note that three would also appear in the BBC film: Ann Robson, David Bowman and Gregory Dempsey, once again in the roles of Mrs Sedley, Ned Keene and Bob Boles. The production was designed

DOI: 10.4324/9781032666631-3

Sadler's Wells Trust Limited
Chairman: David McKenna, O.B.E.

Sadler's Wells Opera
Managing Director and Licensee: Stephen Arlen
Musical Directors: Bryan Balkwill
Mario Bernardi
Directors: Glen Byam Shaw
Edward Renton
Edmund Tracey

Peter Grimes

An Opera by Benjamin Britten

Libretto by Montagu Slater
based on the poem of George Crabbe

By permission of Boosey and Hawkes
Music Publishers Ltd.

Conductor: Bryan Balkwill

Producer: Basil Coleman

Designer: Alan Tagg

Lighting: Charles Bristow

Staff Producer: William Royston

Tuesday, April 11, 1967
32nd performance at Sadler's Wells

'Peter Grimes' was first performed in London at Sadler's Wells Theatre on June 7, 1945. The first performance of this production was at the New Theatre, Oxford on April 23, 1963.

Sadler's Wells Theatre was re-opened by Lilian Baylis on January 6, 1931.

Sadler's Wells Trust Limited works in full association with the Arts Council of Great Britain.

Figure 3.1 Title page of the Sadlers Wells programme for *Peter Grimes* on 11th April 1967.

Source: (Author's collection)

Peter Grimes

Characters:

Peter Grimes, a fisherman	Peter Pears
Ellen Orford, the Borough schoolmistress	Elizabeth Fretwell
Auntie, landlady of The Boar	Sheila Rex
Nieces	Maurine London
	Wendy Baldwin
Balstrode, a retired sea captain	Neil Easton
Mrs. Sedley, a widow	Ann Robson
Swallow, lawyer and magistrate	Noel Mangin
Ned Keen, apothecary	David Bowman
Bob Boles, a Methodist fisherman	Gregory Dempsey
Rector	Francis Egerton
Hobson, the village carrier	Clifford Grant
Dr. Thorpe	Michael Chattin
A Boy, Grimes's new apprentice	Gary Holton
The people of the Borough	

The audience is asked to refrain from applause during the orchestral interludes between the scenes.

Gary Holton and the boys in Act I, appear by kind permission of the Headmaster, The Beaufoy School, Lambeth.

At the Alhambra Theatre, Glasgow, today, Sadler's Wells Opera Company is performing 'La Traviata'.

Figure 3.1a The cast list from the programme for the April 1967 *Peter Grimes*.
Source: (Author's collection)

by Alan Tagg, on lines quite close to those of the original, as far as I could tell from pictures I had seen; the conductor was Bryan Balkwill. Somehow we had managed to get seats in the stalls, but from any seat, the intimacy and power of such a 'big' opera in that relatively modestly proportioned theatre would have been memorable. I shall never forget the impact of the chorus, massed up to the footlights, angrily brandishing their brooms and rakes at us as they cried "*Peter Grimes!. . . . Grimes!*" before scattering to go in search of him. Other great moments included the same chorus marching off to Grimes's hut behind Hobson and his drum towards the end of Act II, Scene 1 ("Bring the branding iron and knife. What's done now is done for life!") before the incomparable quartet of Auntie, the two Nieces and Ellen Orford that inspires Chowrimootoo's measured scorn but never fails to bring tears to my eyes.

Lest I grow prematurely and contentiously sentimental here, I will turn for the moment to the matter of my second encounter with Britten, who had in fact suddenly appeared on stage to take a bow at the end of that performance of *Peter Grimes* on 11th April 1967. He had inserted himself in the centre of the line-up next to Pears, whose hand he took while acknowledging the long-extended and grateful applause. That was my first sight of the composer in the flesh. No less surprising or exciting was the announcement, circulated in the York Music Department early in the following summer term, that he and Pears would be paying a visit in May, when they would give a recital and spend some time in the department; the programme of events to be announced in due course.

Even the most austere of the modernists (their number would grow in subsequent years) clearly felt the excitement and sense of occasion when, as I recall, we assembled in the lecture room in 86 Micklegate. No complete documentation of that visit survives that I am aware of,[2] but the first morning's meeting with them found Wilfrid Mellers 'introducing' Britten and Pears to us (we all, of course, knew what they looked like) and embarrassing them, himself and us in a small way when he began with something like: "Well, Ben and I have been friends for a *long* time, haven't we, Ben? Since when I can't quite remember . . ." He had turned to Britten, as if for an answer, but the latter had simply smiled warmly, covering perhaps a degree of confusion. The moment passed, and our excited anticipation was soon to be richly repaid.

The 'event' that I best recall was to take place next door in the rather small front room of no. 88 Micklegate. We had a star performer in our year, the cellist Moray Welsh, whom Britten had agreed to listen to in a kind of masterclass; he would play the Cello Sonata that Britten had written for Rostropovich in 1961 (in which year the *War Requiem* had also been composed). Those of us who wished to attend were invited to find seats in the rather small room while Moray prepared himself. Our lecturer David Blake had bravely agreed to accompany him, and both were evidently apprehensive. We waited expectantly until the door could be heard opening behind us; Britten was evidently being ushered in to sit somewhere just a row or two back from where I was. The atmosphere was electric. If the two performers were regretting that they had offered to do this, they would at least have known that we were supporting them from our nervous smiles and raised eyebrows.

Silence fell and they began to play. After just a few bars, nerves took their toll, and one or the other became sufficiently lost for the performance to be halted. I think David Blake had just suggested that they start again 'from the top' when the deep, honeyed tones of the composer intervened (we had none of dared to look round): "Look, my fingers are a bit rusty, but would you mind if I *had a go*?" Moray began to eye us with ever-deepening terror as David willingly agreed and Britten had made his way forward and seated himself at the baby grand. We knew of course that Moray could play it, and the performance was soon underway – powerful and captivating. Rusty fingers or not, it became evident that Britten's legendary abilities as an accompanist encouraged Moray to regain his confidence and give his all. Britten had been delighted and had quickly concluded that Moray should, as he told him, go and study *with* Rostropovich and that he would take it upon himself to set arrangements in motion – which he did. Moray subsequently went to Russia to study with the great Russian cellist, in what proved to be a career-launching move.[3]

A more formally presented 'masterclass' must, in fact, have preceded this, back in 86 Micklegate, aimed at singers and given by Peter Pears. I eagerly attended. Tall in bearing and regal in manner, Pears had opened the session by demonstrating a start-up exercise for 'positioning' the voice, in which he stressed the role of the head. He emitted a series of notes, increasing in volume, to a sort of 'ah' sound. His familiar voice, imitable because so individual, was extraordinary at such close quarters, and it filled the room and seemed to make the windows rattle and my ears buzz. That alone has stayed with me, although I have a suspicion that one of our sopranos sang some Purcell, possibly accompanied by Robert Sherlaw Johnson; I imagine that Peter Aston – my first-year tutor and director of the departmental chamber choir – would have been there too.

The glitzy excitement of their visit continued out at the university's still-new Heslington campus. It might have been early afternoon, where a more public 'Meet Britten and Pears' sort of event had been arranged. It was run as a relatively informal question-and-answer session and was well attended, both by us and by interested members of the wider university and its administrative staff. The location was a large panelled room in the fine old house (Heslington Hall) in whose grounds the university had been (and was still being) built. It was filled with sunlight, and Britten and Pears sat behind a table at the front, looking deeply tanned and relaxed.[4] They spoke fluently and well, and the audience responded with grateful warmth that seemed appropriate to the spring afternoon whose calm surface was disturbed only slightly by two of the public questions that I remember. The first had come early, from the wife of one of the university's senior administrators, herself a singer. I paraphrase her question as best I can from a distance of over half a century:

> Close relationships between composers and singers seem quite rare, but yours has been so successful and productive. Could you perhaps tell us how you first got together?

We, the music students, were all sufficiently well-versed in 'the open secret' to shrink down slightly in our seats in sympathetic embarrassment. What would Britten, who was at that point speaking for both of them, say? It was rather straightforward:

> Peter, you are so much better at this sort of thing than I am, and you remember more. Would you like to deal with this one?

Pears took it up with the barest moment for reflection and without the slightest hint of embarrassment, and began to detail early performances in which they had both been involved, and works that Ben had then written for him. Nothing to frighten the horses, as they say, just a calm rehearsal of facts and places – with Britten occasionally chipping in. We breathed, I think, a silently shared sigh of relief and were impressed by how deftly Pears had told the tale. Other questions included one about Britten's affection (or not) for music of the past, and for 'great composers' like Beethoven. He might well have said something about Purcell and his English forbears, but on Beethoven specifically, some thoughtfully discriminating comments were followed by an amusing aside: "But he did make some *very* nasty noises." A final moment of awkwardness had involved a rather bland music education graduate (I think), who had clearly been reading Wilfrid and had asked a more specifically challenging question of Britten, the burden of which was:

> Why are so many of your works about the death of innocence?

To this Britten's response was rather brief and just a little frosty:

> Oh I never think about my works in that sort of way, and could really not comment very usefully.

He might have added: "Perhaps that's for you to tell *me*?", but memory no longer serves. What I do recall is that we all soon trooped out through French doors into the gardens at the back of Heslington Hall, as the session ended. Somehow I managed to position myself beside Britten in the approach to the door and eagerly asked a question which I now rather regret:

> What do you think about Boulez and integral serialism?

I nevertheless relished his reply:

> Well I think one can go too far with that sort of thing . . .

It was my one moment of conversation with Britten, with heart beating fast as we came out into the sunshine. He then walked over to Henry Moore's seated King and Queen (the big bronze sculpture has since been removed) and appreciatively stroked the knee of the king as he responded in a calm and relaxed way to further questions and comments that were eagerly put to him in front of the great clipped yews on that memorable day.

* * *

The most formal and public part of the visit[5] had been the recital Britten and Pears gave at 8.00 pm in Derwent College Hall. We knew it as the dining room in the only other college then completed, next to Langwith, at the Heslington Hall end of the great artificial lake that would one day be surrounded by other colleges and university buildings. The date was Tuesday 9th May 1967, and Britten's big concert Steinway had had to be manoeuvred into place on the low platform. My cherished, typed-out programme reminds me that they began with a set of ten Schubert songs (including 'Auf dem Wasser zu singen' and 'Nacht und Träume'). It continued with Britten's *Six Hölderlin Fragments* (Op. 61) and ended with his Pushkin cycle *The Poet's Echo* (Op. 76) from 1958 and 1965 respectively.

We were lost in admiration; of Pears, of course, but no less of Britten's discreetly masterful style of accompaniment, indeed of being 'the accompanist' – looking carefully up at Pears for starting cues and at no point playing 'over' him, mostly leaning in to the keyboard, the focussed and modestly absorbed professional. I suspect that there must have been a folksong arrangement or two by way of encores, but it was above all one of those rare events when we students, I think, for the most part, simply relished the thought of relishing later (as I do now) the fact that we had 'been there'.

Essay: *Grimes* and the Sentimental

I must nevertheless return to the matter of *Peter Grimes* and my first live experience of it in that memorable Sadler's Wells revival of April 1967. Might it in any way illuminate Chowrimootoo's examination of Britten's operas in relation to the concept of 'middlebrow modernism'? I have already alluded to the very opening of his book, the Acknowledgements. I am generously named there, but must recall once more his opening gambit of personalizing his project in the odd, revealing way that he chooses, confirming – for no immediately obvious reason – that his "austere, modernist exterior" conceals "a sentimentality as sickly as anything in *Peter Grimes*."

I turned earlier to Britten himself for expressions of the kind of outwardly highbrow modernist superiority about 'sickly sentimentality' that Chowrimootoo's study mostly cites as directed *against* him. A recurring touchstone of what modernists and critics like Joseph Kerman have scorned as examples of operatic sentimentality[6] is identified by Chowrimootoo in Richard Strauss's *Der Rosenkavalier*. He mentions its supposedly middlebrow-pleasing set pieces, like the final Trio, in mildly ironic, unflattering comparison with the Act II women's quartet in *Peter Grimes*. And then there is the *Rosenkavalier* overture which would, he reminds us, have highbrow novelist Iris Murdoch's character Bradley Pearson (in *The Black Prince*, 1973) rushing out of the Royal Opera House to be sick after suffering its explicitly orgasmic excess (actually one of Strauss's naughtiest and most 'modern' of parodic jokes). I would once again beg to point out that Britten had got there first. Accompanist Graham Johnson recalled an awkward Red House dinner with the composer and Peter Pears and others in 1971. His account of an exchange with Britten about *Der Rosenkavalier* was included in Humphrey Carpenter's biography of the composer:

> B.B.: It is utterly loathsome. I almost get sick listening to it – even the overture makes me physically sick.
> G.J.: But it's got so many beautiful things in it, hasn't it?
> B.B.: What do you like about it?
> G.J.: Well that Trio (*singing unwisely*) 'Marie Thérèse . . .'
> B.B.: (*utterly icily*) I know how it goes, thank you very much, and I don't need you to sing it to me!
> (*Horrible silence. Close examination of plate-ware by other guests. Peter activates the foot bell for Heather to bring the next course.*)[7]

One thing is clear from this. If Britten was, in Chowrimootoo's sense, a creator and purveyor of some form of 'middlebrow modernism', his general stance, even in private, remained that of a decidedly highbrow modernist of the period, whose distaste for *Der Rosenkavalier* could be expressed in terms no less vituperative than those adopted by modernists of other cliques and clans when describing *his* music. The conclusion must surely be that all such terms demand to be studied in relation to what their users intend to achieve by mobilizing them within a particular historical and cultural context. As 'style categories' in the old, Adlerian or conventional musicological sense they are of doubtful if any use. While you might advertise your affiliation to musical 'modernism' by carefully avoiding or challenging the long-shared grammar and expressive vocabulary of tonality, the stylistic signs of 'middlebrow' sensibility, usually recognized in modes of reception (not least like my own), prove surely too varied and interesting to submit to a single label, given what we learn about them from their systematically attempted critical erasure by Chowrimootoo's anxiety about 'sentiment' or 'emotion' in all their various guises.

The point is reinforced somewhat by a ventured explanation of the term 'middlebrow' by Chowrimootoo and Kate Guthrie, in the introduction to their 'Colloquy: Musicology and the Middlebrow' in the summer 2020 edition of the *Journal of the American Musicological Society*, where the possibly 'unfashionable' implications of the term are countered with a clear-sounding definition:

> Coined in the 1920s to describe those who fell between high and low culture, the concept harks back to an era openly invested in cultural hierarchies.[8]

This seems to reinforce the suspicion that the term only ever had meaning as a buzzword in a mode of historically contextualized *discourse* that was as much about cultural cliques, camps and class as about literary or musical 'style' – at least in any sense that could transcend the sort of "thick" history to whose embrace Chowrimootoo claims to have been encouraged by Professor Roger Parker. The latter's scepticism about "composer-centred-monographs" is something the former seems nevertheless to have ignored.[9] He is of course allowed to, not least by me, but the strange complexity of the result is nowhere more clearly revealed than in his chapter on *Peter Grimes*, whose full title is 'Sentimentality under Erasure in *Peter Grimes*'. A dangerous one, perhaps, given the opening line of the author's Acknowledgements. If my understanding is right that 'middlebrow' is a historical category primarily referencing actual or suspected modes of *reception*, then the question arises whether it might better have been called 'Sentimentality under Erasure in Critical *Readings* of *Peter Grimes*'?

The term 'sentimentality' urgently merits further thought. It is never really defined or questioned in his book, even where it is specifically marked out as 'sickly', as in the case of *Peter Grimes*. In his chapter on the opera, Chowrimootoo does, however, cite I. A. Richards ("one of the torchbearers of modernist criticism"[10]) on sentimentality both as a "mode of reception"[11] and also as an "affliction" (Chowrimootoo's term[12]) that can be recognized "if it is too great for the occasion."[13] But it is difficult to define something as an excess of itself, when that self remains opaque, although Chowrimootoo adds a further gloss derived from Richards, that sentimentality is to be recognized as evidence of "a crudeness of emotion, quite separate from its intensity"[14] or possibly (Chowrimootoo paraphrases) evincing "a certain narrowness of vision, as if viewing art and the world through rose-tinted spectacles."[15] Here he is citing Richards's *Practical Criticism: A Study of Judgement* (1929). There seems to be considerable slippage and implicit dissonance between emotional 'crudeness', 'narrowness' and rose-tinted, presumably 'romantic' idealization. It is a pity that Chowrimootoo did not thicken his history still further at this point and consult the partly admiring but rigorously probing consideration of Richards by Raymond Williams in his *Culture and Society 1780–1950*, published in 1958. It post-dates *Peter Grimes* by just over a decade, but Williams's consideration of Richards, alongside F. R. Leavis, in the fourth chapter of the second part of his study, valuably proposes the following (we might think of 'ordinary' and 'literary' here as sporting imaginary scare-quotes):

> Richards's account of the inadequacy of ordinary response when compared with the adequacy of literary response is a cultural symptom rather than a diagnosis.[16]

In other words, it might have been Richards's problem, rather than the ordinary responder's. Williams concluded:

> All that Richards has taught us about language and communication, and for which we acknowledge our debt, has to be reviewed, finally, when we

have rid ourselves of the vestiges of Aesthetic Man – alone in a hostile environment, receiving and organizing his experiences – which Richards, even as brilliant opponent, in fact inherited.[17]

Much might be said about Raymond Williams (1921–1988), as a near contemporary of Britten. His frequently reprinted *Culture and Society* – essentially a history of the idea of Culture and the role of 'art' within it – moved on from Richards and Leavis to explore a Marxist perspective. There he questioned the usefulness of the notion of 'bourgeois culture' as necessarily opposed to the 'proletarian', and moved to outline a vision of a society whose functional concept of culture might look beyond the rigidity of conventional 'class' divisions and the 'ladder-to-climb' metaphor for social betterment. We needed, he suggested, to confront the contemporary problem of democracy at the end of the 1950s and its "dominative attitude to communication" in which leaders seemed "genuinely afraid of trusting the process of majority discussion and decision." On these grounds they embraced 'brow' mentality and its accompanying demarcations and quasi-ethical erasures (as I might put it now, with Chowrimootoo's Britten study beside my copy of the Williams).[18] Strikingly, and relevantly in this case, Williams notes with concern that as a critical strategy, the "whole theory of mass communication depends, essentially, on a minority in some way exploiting a majority."[19]

Much, he suggests, hinges upon whether we think of that majority (and its tastes and preferences) objectively as a 'mass' or more tendentiously as a 'mob'. Should mass democracy mean 'mob rule'? – and should we accept that implicit 'othering' of the masses? Is that othering, indeed, what highbrow modernism was often engaged in doing, I now ask, with its consequent invention of the category 'middlebrow' to catch would-be highbrows who didn't, they felt, quite belong in their midst? Williams worries seriously about glibly figuring the masses (now perhaps including the middlebrow) as representing a manipulated and manipulatable 'mob', which would hold them to be deserving ("in a good cause") to be addressed "at a level of communication which our experience and training tell us is inferior." Should we therefore 'talk down', for all that we might believe idealistically in democracy? Should we be prepared to accept the implicit self-imposed requirement to "cheapen our own experience and to adulterate the common language" – as if to *maintain* social difference?[20]

I wonder whether there might not, indeed, be a problematically *modernist* way of doing the latter (in a back-to-front version of the same 'good cause'?). If so, questions about 'middlebrow' should urgently be reduced to questions about what *highbrow* might really be and mean. What, more explicitly, might be revealed is how modernism *colluded* with the exclusion of the supposedly middlebrow. It is significant that Chowrimootoo himself, towards the end of his chapter on *Peter Grimes* – having for a time more or less avoided both 'middlebrow' and 'sentimental' as decisive terms – seems to perform a *volte-face*, turning from the put-downs and erasures of modernist/middlebrow critical discourse in the period to accept that if he were, after all, to position

Peter Grimes as in some way 'modernist', he would be seen to be carrying out a strategy that could be defined as "a rhetorical performance that depended for its effect on the very sentimentality it rejected."[21]

If *Grimes* might tendentiously (and, I would argue, unconvincingly) be interpreted as itself performing such rejections or 'erasures', Chowrimootoo seems nevertheless to have opened up the possibility that the critique might be turned back upon the critics. For which reason we are confronted once more by that vexed and vexing term 'sentimental'. Raymond Williams's own treatment of it in his later book *Keywords* (1975, revised 1983) is worth considering. This came in a section on the history of the now largely disappeared term 'sensibility', which in the eighteenth-century, he suggests, moved from a meaning rather "like that of modern *awareness*" to something stronger, implying "the ability to feel":

> It was at this point that its relation to *sentimental* became important. . . . The association with *sensibility* was then close: a conscious openness to feelings and also a conscious consumption of feelings. The latter made *sentimental* vulnerable. . . . Much that was moral or radical in intention and in effect, was washed with the same brush that was used to depict self-conscious or self-indulgent displays of *sentiment*. Southey, in his conservative phase, brought the words together: "the sentimental classes, persons of ardent or morbid sensibility" (1823). This complaint is against people who feel "too much" as well as against those who "indulge their emotions." This confusion has permanently damaged *sentimental* (though limited positive uses survive, typically in *sentimental value*) and wholly determined *sentimentality*.[22]

Emboldened by the liberating implications of this perspective on 'sentimentality' as a term potentially recoverable for a wide range of forms of emotional response to, and engagement with, experience in general as much as to art more specifically, I am bound to 'come out' in my response to Chowrimootoo not simply in the now-conventional terms of sexual politics but more precisely and no less proudly as a 'middlebrow sentimentalist'. I am happy to consider myself one in whom a wide range of richly welcome sentiments aroused by *Peter Grimes* – sometimes disturbed and disturbing, at others profoundly consoling – converged in my reception of it in 1967 and ever after, less as 'modernist' performance, in the tensely self-constraining and self-'erasing' way that Chowrimootoo seeks to outline (at least up until the final sentence of his chapter on it), than as rather gloriously *anti*-modernist in its practical refusal of the apologetically self-censoring modernist hang-ups that a work like *Wozzeck* perhaps more famously and convincingly exhibits. There was, I would argue, a striking distinction between the highbrow, high-modernist critical utterances of the socially aware younger Britten and his much more subversively liberal compositional practice, particularly in a work like *Peter Grimes*.

I have already recalled the powerful effect of the chorus in that 1967 revival in the relatively intimate space of the Sadlers Wells Theatre. Let me return to that moment in Act III, with the enraged inhabitants of the Borough massed at the footlights, brandishing their home-made weapons and calling out "Peter Grimes!" – we know they are now well on the way to becoming a lynch mob. Metaphorically, if not actually, it remains a gloriously hair-raising example of what I might call the operatic-choral sublime. I am thinking here of the old Romantic meaning of that term 'sublime' as embracing a beauty that is also terrible and even fear-inducing.

By way of comparison, I turn here to an opera even less welcoming of austere modernists, or more welcoming of seekers after middlebrow sensation and sensibility (in a generously post-Raymond Williams, re-purposed understanding of that term). We have not been long immersed in a garish, fantastically re-imagined ancient China, when the chorus of 'People', in Puccini's posthumous *Turandot* (1926), greedy for terror and retribution before the gates of what we would now call Beijing's 'Forbidden City', demonstrate their readiness to behave like the devotees of ex-President Trump, as a crowd that could even turn into a 'mob'. The Mandarin has announced that the Prince of Persia, the latest suitor of the Princess Turandot, had failed his scary Trial by Riddle and must therefore die. The chorus accept their servile role and support the death sentence with mounting enthusiasm:

People: Die! Yes die!
         We want the executioner.
         To the scaffold! Let him die!

Their bloodthirsty relish is nevertheless immediately repelled by the palace guards, who nervously *fear insurrection*, something out of their control, and bear down upon them:

Guards: Back, dogs! Back!

Many are knocked over, including the deposed King of the Tartars, whose female servant fights to save him from being trampled. They too have become victims as a great theme seems to come from nowhere to sweep down upon them from the orchestra like an avenging angel, blazing its tonal ambivalence between F-sharp minor and A major. It is a sort of Narrator's Intervention that throws our expectations, our sympathies and scruples back at us in an unforgettable moment of the operatic-choral sublime: we have been manipulated into enthusiastic complicity with cruelty, only now, in our turn, to be condemned for the unruly implications of that very enthusiasm. The operatic moment embraces the comprehension that in a society dependent upon rabble-rousing, both rabble and rousers are literally threatened by unsentimental enthusiasm – which therefore reveals sentimentality's aspect and potential as a form of liberation.

A strikingly comparable effect, albeit in rather different dramatic circumstances, is what had raised my hair in the 1967 revival of *Peter Grimes*. Before the chorus shout out Grimes's name, there had been the long *stretto* build-up of overlapping canonic insistence that "Him who despises us, we'll destroy." It leads to a tremendous climax when the excitement of shared outrage, seeded with growing vindictive bitterness by Mrs Sedley and her 'suspicions', binds the "townspeople and fisherfolk"[23] into a single-willed malevolent mob whose members are suddenly required to utter a series of crazed, non-verbal "Ha, ha ha's." But this is no laughing matter, no simple mocking taunt; instead, we hear a sudden, quite unexpected, full-choral, lyrical homophonic delivery of a little phrase from some of the on-stage dance-music that had earlier formed a background to Mrs Sedley's unburdening of her suspicions to Ned Keene. Singing that phrase to the single syllable of 'Ha', the chorus now glissando upwards to participate in one of those Puccinian moments of the operatic-choral sublime as they turn the silly little dance tune into a *fortissimo, molto largamente* melodic rainbow of triumphant certainty that is chilling, in one sense, even as it must blow the socks off any but the most austerely insensitive modernist audience member. We suddenly see and feel 'with' the chorus, even as we grasp the inhumanity and brutality of their purpose (noting that selected male voices – Swallow, Hobson and the chorus basses – add the words "We'll make the murderer pay for his crime!" in the final bars of this climax before the cries of "Peter Grimes!"). We become part of the mob, and must live to regret it, even as we recall it as one of the great moments of grand opera.

This hardly merits the mealy-mouthed epithet 'sentimental'. The term seems, indeed, to have no more relevance to the complexity of the opera's central character – admittedly already haloed in 1967 with enthusiastic expectation before he sang a single note, given that Pears himself was recreating the role. The difference between the Grimes of Britten's opera and Crabbe's in *The Borough* has understandably occasioned much comment. Philip Brett played a significant role in uncovering the archaeological layers of the libretto's history, during which Grimes the sadistic misfit fisherman became, with Montagu Slater's initial connivance, gradually transformed into something quite other than the anti-hero of a "rather gloomy homosexual bloodthirsty melodrama" (here Brett was adding his own gloss on Britten's fears about the subject that he had expressed to Christopher Isherwood in 1942, without alluding to the matter of Grimes's possibly implied sexuality[24]). The transformation seems to have gone far enough, in Britten's and Pears's rather radical later modifications of the role, for Slater to publish his libretto in 1946 as he might have wanted it. Brett suspects that Britten and Pears moved away from his high-principled Marxist-orientated 'realism' towards a more centre-left political position, perhaps pandering to an audience they did not want to alienate too comprehensively.[25]

With hindsight, their pruning and focussing of the text seems mostly to have achieved clarity and a more characteristically 'operatic' economy, although the evidence that they still alienated their more conservative critics is clear in stories about the vexed and embattled preparations for the premiere and about the subsequently celebrated no. 38 bus conductor. He seems to have been heard calling out, as they neared the theatre: "Any more for Peter Grimes, the sadistic fisherman!"[26] One might imagine that the 'sadistic fisherman' tag could have been maliciously spread in 1945 by members of the disgruntled group of musicians from the Sadlers Wells company who objected to having to participate in "such a piece of cacophony," with perhaps unspoken innuendo about Britten and Pears having been Conscientious Objectors. They might have been at one with my uncle's memorable anti-modernist distaste for "that kind of thing," recently arrived home, as he would have been, from the war.[27]

They, like others of the early critics, clearly took *Peter Grimes* to be (and may even have *heard* it as) 'modernism' of the aggressively nasty, foreign kind (austerity really didn't come into it). As a result, its evident success with large parts of the audience had to be accommodated, if not actually celebrated, by many of those same critics. Before fully revealing his concern about cultural evasion and escapism, directly addressed at the start of his chapter on *Albert Herring*, Chowrimootoo suggests here that the evident success of *Grimes* with the audience presented those potentially hostile critics with a particular kind of problem:

> With these images of rich and poor, admirals and bus conductors, coming together to cheer Britten's opera enthusiastically, *Grimes* appeared to bring wartime images of national unity and solidarity into a postwar future.
>
> In leading with these hyperbolic discussions and vignettes, commentators were seeking both to do justice to and to justify their emotive responses. Yet even the most enthusiastic critics were anxious about the propriety of these responses. At a time when fears about cultural commodification were high, the bus conductor's treatment of the opera as a tourist attraction threatened the boundaries between art and commerce.[28]

There, of course, spoke High Modernism and speaks peculiarly in Chowrimootoo's description of the commentators seeking to justify "their emotive responses." This apparently incorrect word substitution (emot*i*ve for emotion*al*) could itself be a form of the technique of 'erasure' which Chowrimootoo seeks to discern within the opera, as if trying to rescue it for Modernism of a confused kind – as if it and the Verdian models of musical drama that Britten might have acknowledged (to which I would add the Puccinian and even Purcellian) were not and had not been threatening the boundaries between art and commerce for some time! Emotional responses, escapism, excess and all the messy other things that opera facilitates have been what both patrons and audiences *paid for*. Of *course*, highbrow modernist idealists frowned upon it: for the same reasons that Pierre Boulez would later famously propose blowing up opera houses.

Thus soiled and mired, I return from the battlefield to my own experience, as an enthusiastic paying audience-member of that production in 1967. It is relevant in its small way, perhaps, to understanding why *Grimes* struck me as liberatingly *anti*-modernist: not erasing the emotional, but *being* 'emotive' – giving richly of all that the high modernists who would soon be dominating the 'creativity' agenda back in the York Music Department might have rejected, in spite of Wilfrid Mellers's taste for Britten (along with all the rest) and his keen understanding of *Peter Grimes*. That was succinctly expressed in his chapter on 'Europe Today' in the fourth volume (*Romanticism and the 20th Century*) of *Man and His Music* (1962), whose fat, one-volume edition I had received as a requested birthday present from my parents while I was still at school, probably in 1964 – the year of its second impression):

> *Peter Grimes* turns on the ancient myth of the Savage Man who in Eden would be innate goodness; whom the depravity of humanity renders destructive. Deprived of Ellen's love, Grimes's innocence turns to cruelty and he destroys the boy who is his own soul. The World (thrillingly represented by the chorus) rounds on him and harries him to his death.[29]

This neatly presents two significant observations. The first is that Grimes himself is a tragic victim, a misfit who becomes a kind of martyr (in a sense *with* his two apprentices who die): a self-condemning victim of the "thrilling" chorus of "townspeople and fisherfolk." Unsentimentally, and at times *negatively* portrayed, their vindictive and violent rejection of the outsider fisherman is unflinchingly represented (here Mellers's second significant observation) as characteristic of a manipulated, even self-manipulating 'mob'. Only Ellen and the 'fallen' women – themselves marginalized by the folksy patriarchy – really understand and might be able to pardon the rest of their community, for whom such pardon might seem neither deserved nor relevant.

All this was famously emphasized in Pears's idiosyncratic performance. In 1967 he was already approaching 60 and looked for all the world like a kindly headmaster trying to act the part of a wilder and presumably younger fisherman in order to teach us something. I say this affectionately, rather than satirically, since part of what he seemed to be teaching the audience that night was indeed that his Grimes was much closer to Mellers's than to Crabbe's, or even, perhaps, Slater's. In 1965 Pears himself described Grimes as "a mixed-up 'modern' character and not an old-fashioned cruel villain."[30] He certainly had the music: music that was not afraid to utilize the shared language and inherited gestures of the old tonal ways, in however original and 'modern'-feeling a fashion. It's there already in the staged Prologue, where we are thrown straight in to a rather jolly and jocular type of musical 'new objectivity', with Lawyer Swallow opening the Coroner's Inquest to investigate the death of Grimes's apprentice. His clearly enunciated recitative seems rhythmically to owe more to the Broadway Britten had hoped to win over with *Paul Bunyan* than to conventional modes of European operatic recitative. But as soon as Grimes repeats "I swear by Almighty God," we feel that he understands what that oath might mean – and *means* it, indeed, as Swallow's skittish wind and brass give way to romantic strings. They quietly sustain a simple dominant seventh chord in G major against Swallow's peremptorily gritty chord of A-flat major with added dissonant G natural. The effect is of a kind of musical 'halo' technique that dates back to Bach's passions; Grimes's chord is eloquently presented in the Vocal Score accompaniment as a perfect fifth in the left hand (D and A) with the devilish tritone (the C and F-sharp of the later *War Requiem*) in the right.

Although his chances really to 'sing' in the Prologue are restricted, we learn what he can do in its beautiful closing duet with Ellen Orford, '*Recitativo (senza misura)*' – she with a key signature of four sharps, he with four flats (E major against F minor/A-flat major). It dramatizes her calming influence against his anger at the Borough's hatred and newly reinforced reason to gossip, when finally they converge. They briefly unite in musical unison in the passage that begins with a quiet, skywards-rising minor ninth straight out of late Mahler and ends in 'her' key of E major, which will be taken up in the high violins and flutes, as if from a far horizon, descending with little downward runs suggesting bird cries. These inaugurate the first of the great 'Sea Interludes', here unmistakably evoking the seashore, with gently upwards bubbling waves – like arpeggios, but of consecutive thirds – a musical image of extraordinary 'found' simplicity, yet utterly original: something that, once heard, is never forgotten.

Grimes's peculiar musical eloquence has its finest moment, perhaps, when, after the impressive 'storm' Interlude (which still strikes me as alluding almost deliberately to the no less tempestuous, more explicitly subjective 'storm' of the Finale of Mahler's First Symphony), he bursts into The Boar like a creature from another world. Weather-beaten but without oilskins, he intervenes in a tipsy gathering of sheltering locals. They greet his appearance by ceasing all conversation and muttering "Talk of the devil and there he is." Grimes had come to pick up his new apprentice but has evidently been distracted by a vision he has had of stars glimpsed beyond and between the departing storm clouds:

> Now the Great Bear and Pleiades
>   Where earth moves
> Are drawing up the clouds
>   Of human grief
> [. . .]
> Who can turn skies back and begin again?

Hardly a question for a crowded night in the pub. . . Grimes brings with him poetry, philosophy and a quite different kind of music to that employed by Balstrode earlier to instil a communal spirit after things had got rather boisterous. He also brings the orchestra whose accompaniment sinks, or drifts diatonically downwards in successive stages beneath Grimes's initial words, delivered on a monotone. Small wonder that his aria, which stops time and encourages not 'sentimentality' but vision, awe, sorrow and compassion, leads the uncomprehending locals to assume that "he's mad, or drunk" and edge towards violence against him. It is quelled only by Ned Keene taking a leaf out of Balstrode's book and striking up a round in which all can join.

It shouldn't work – but it does, thanks to Britten's keen sense of timing and how to stage his dramatic effects musically. I am not sure how well I knew the opera before that night, but I certainly possessed the 1959 recording, with its flimsy booklet of notes and no libretto. I no less certainly knew it well enough in 1967 to recall fixing my gaze on that rear-stage door into The Boar where I knew Grimes/Pears would soon appear, before singing "Now the Great Bear and Pleiades . . ." It seemed to me that I had a duty to remember this, and that a time would come when others might envy my having seen it – rather as I had envied Hans Redlich when he had visited the York department, at the invitation of Wilfrid, who had encouraged him to retell for us his memory of being taken by his father (as a 6-year-old in Vienna) to see Mahler's funeral procession pass by.

Britten had not been a central preoccupation for me at that time when, like others of my contemporaries, I was busy concentrating on the mysteries of mediaeval music while working my way carefully, and with greater commitment, through the early works of Schoenberg, which I was discovering with almost fanatical engagement. But given my early experience of *Noye's Fludde*, *The Turn of the Screw* and the *War Requiem*, it took little work that Easter to prepare myself for the revival of *Peter Grimes*, from which my friend and I emerged breathless, with stinging hands, hoarse throats and moist eyes. At that time, my uncle aside, I knew little of the anti-Britten modernists (although I soon would) and was simply confirmed in the realization that I needed to know more, and that operas, Britten's not least, were probably going to occupy me for years to come.

Notes

1 The phrase is John Bridcut's, indeed the title of the book he published in 2006, derived from his BBC documentary of the same name, first broadcast in 2004. See John Bridcut, *Britten's Children* (London: Faber & Faber, 2006).
2 In fact my contemporary Moray Welsh, who features in what follows, has written a memoir of his own that deals with this visit. He has kindly allowed me to see the relevant portion, which has enabled me to correct some of my own faulty memories; only in few details do our recollections significantly differ. Moray's account indicates that the recital Britten and Pears gave on this occasion was almost certainly the first event of the visit – and would have taken place on the evening *before* the events here recorded.

3 Moray's own account times this performance as taking place at 12.30pm, before which he had had to make a rushed trip across to Leeds to fetch a copy of the score, with the piano part, from the City library (presumably he had a cellist's copy without the full accompaniment). His account also suggests that Pears's masterclass would have taken place *before* this, although his recollection that his own performance with Britten was supported by a 'couple of friends' expands in my own to something between eight and ten of us, perhaps more. He makes it clear that David Blake was in fact heroically attempting to sight-read the piano part.
4 The precise chronology is unclear here. Moray Welsh recalls a reception after the recital (probably on the previous evening) which took place in Heslington Hall. I do not recall that, and may well have missed it. But at the event I describe Britten and Pears were certainly not in concert-attire, being smart but 'casually' dressed.
5 As indicated above, I defer to Moray's conviction that this was, in fact, the *initial* event of the visit. Vol. Six (1966–76) of the *Letters from a Life: The Selected Letters of Benjamin Britten 1913–1976* (Woodbridge: The Boydell Press in association with the Britten-Pears Foundation, 2012), 116 (note 4) makes it clear that their next recital in Richmond (N. Yorks) was on 11 May. The other events I describe must therefore have happened on 10 May, with Britten and Pears departing late-afternoon that day for Richmond.
6 Kerman found the Marschallin "unappetizing" because she "indulges her sentimentality so consciously", adding "No one who understood *The Marriage of Figaro* could ever have taken *Der Rosenkavalier* seriously . . .". See Joseph Kerman, *Opera as Drama*, revised edition (London: Faber & Faber, 1989), Ch. 10., 209–10 and 211.
7 Carpenter, *Benjamin Britten*, 518.
8 Christopher Chowrimootoo and Kate Guthrie (convenors), 'Colloquy: Musicology and the Middlebrow', *Journal of the American Musicological Society*, Vol. 72, 2 (Summer 2020), 327.
9 See Chowrimootoo, *Middlebrow Modernism*, x.
10 Ibid., 32.
11 Ibid., 45.
12 Ibid., 32.
13 Ibid., citing I.A. Richards, *Practical Criticism: A Study of Judgement* (London: Routledge & Kegan Paul, 1929).
14 Ibid, citing the same source.
15 Ibid.
16 Raymond Williams, *Culture and Society 1780–1950* (London: Penguin Books in association with Chatto & Windus, 1963 [first published 1958]), 245.
17 Ibid, 246. By 'Aesthetic Man' Williams references earlier ideas of the Artist as a 'revealer' of truth and beauty whose 'goodness' was opposed to the pleasures and preoccupations of a corrupt society which it (and he) might theoretically improve.
18 Ibid., 303.
19 Ibid.

20 Ibid., 294.
21 Chowrimootoo, *Middlebrow Modernism*, 62.
22 Raymond Williams, *Keywords. A Vocabulary of Culture and Society*, revised and expanded Flamingo edition (London: [originally Fontana 1976] Fontana, 1983), 281–2. (The original also uses bold typeface for the 'key' word in the relevantly titled section, which here was 'sensibility').
23 I quote from the list of 'Characters' in the Boosey & Hawkes libretto: *Peter Grimes. An Opera in Three Acts and a Prologue*, words by Montagu Slater, Music by Benjamin Britten (London: Boosey & Hawkes [1945], revised version 1961), 1.
24 See Brett's essay '*Peter Grimes*': The Growth of the Libretto' in Paul Banks (ed.), *The Making of Peter Grimes. Essays and Studies, Aldeburgh Studies in Music*, Vol. 6 (Woodbridge: The Boydell Press and The Britten Estate Ltd., 1996 [paperback reissue 2000]), 53–78 (the quotation comes from 62). Brett had famously been the first to address directly the question of *Grimes* and homosexuality in his article 'Britten and Grimes' in *The Musical Times*, December 1977, Vol. 118, 1618, 995–1000.
25 For his own published libretto, see Montagu Slater, *Peter Grimes and Other Poems* (London: John Lane the Bodley Head, 1946). In Act II, scene 3 (Slater, 42–4) Grimes is certainly tougher on the boy than in the opera.
26 Carpenter, *Benjamin Britten*, 224.
27 On the singers' attempted rebellion about this "piece of cacophony", see Ibid., 219.
28 Chowrimootoo, *Middlebrow Modernism*, 31.
29 Alec Harman (with Anthony Milner) and Wilfrid Mellers, *Man and His Music. The Story of Musical Experience in the West* (London: Barrie & Rockliff, 1962/64), 1043 ['Romanticism and the Twentieth Century', Ch. 9, 'Europe Today'].
30 Peter Pears, 'Peter Grimes' (requested, but apparently not published, for a Metropolitan Opera publication in 1965), Paul Banks (ed.), *The Making of Peter Grimes*, 5. See Note 24 above.

4 Graduation: Britten and Pears Return to York

After the close encounters of our exciting first year at York, Britten fell more into the background of the musical landscape of our second and third. I had become a 'Pure Music' student, and there were things to catch up on and work to be done. Traditional Harmony and Counterpoint tutorials continued in all three years, along with Aural Tests; both were part of our Final Examinations in 1969. There was also a certain amount of the free composition that Wilfrid wanted us all to produce, while contributing to the rich and busy series of departmental performance activities (I played the double bass in the University Orchestra, conducted by David Blake). I was also, all through those last two undergraduate years, a devoted and rather proud member of the department's Chamber Choir, directed by Peter Aston, under whom we memorably learnt the two big Britten works that had failed to impress me as a schoolboy: *Hymn to St Cecelia* and *Rejoice in the Lamb*.

The absence of any further personal appearances of Britten and Pears in York during those years was made up for by their memorable return at the very end of our final year in 1969. This had seen the completion and opening of the Lyons Concert Hall, with its attached wing of teaching, practice, library and office spaces to house the department in newly comfortable and modern surroundings. The whole complex overlooked the lake at Heslington, just beyond the still-new Vanbrugh College.[1] Britten and Pears played no part in the busy inaugural March 'Music Week', in which there were numerous concerts by ourselves and various guest performers (like Frances Jackson putting the new organ through its paces, Raphael Orozco giving a piano recital and the BBC Northern Symphony Orchestra playing Wagner and Messiaen (the latter's *Le reveil des oiseaux* with our own Robert Sherlaw Johnson as pianist). They did, however, return in May to give a memorable performance of the complete *Winterreise* of Schubert, this time in the new Lyons Concert Hall.

It had originally been billed as a Celebrity Concert in the University's Central Hall, which would have held more people (the concert was advertised as "in aid of the University Appeal"), but that building would have been far less acoustically appropriate for what was another memorably intimate occasion. Once again Britten's big Steinway concert grand had arrived in a mighty removal van; its installation was now more easily facilitated by the purpose-built external doors that afforded direct access to the new hall from the parking area. The concert was as impressive as expected, with Britten once again exercising his discreet yet unmistakable mastery as an accompanist. It was a meticulously crafted and paced performance. They had, of course, recorded the cycle in 1965; in retrospect, the closing lines of 'Der Leiermann' seemed to raise a touching question about their professional, and perhaps personal, relationship. William Mann's translation in the programme put it thus:

> Strange old fellow, shall I go with you?
> Will you grind your organ to my singing?

This was also to be the fateful year in which the Snape Maltings would burn down, just a few weeks after that performance, on the first day (7th June) of the Aldeburgh Festival. The chaotic rearrangement of the festival venues, followed by the anxious quest for the funding and rebuilding of the Maltings (heroically achieved in time for the following year's festival) makes all the more remarkable the dim recollection, confirmed by contemporaries and a photograph that Moray Welsh managed to have taken of himself between them, that Britten and Pears were in fact both present at our graduation ceremony on Tuesday, 15th July. One of the University's online archives of graduation ceremonies and honorary degree recipients lists Sir Peter Pears as having received an honorary degree on that day – appropriate not least for the *Winterreise* concert having been so generously donated to the University. That Britten accompanied Pears added lustre indeed to our celebration of the completion of our degree course as one of the privileged, state-funded generations of 'Britten's children' now about to find our way in the world.

Essay: *Billy Budd*: Confronting the Highbrow Critique of Opera

Britten and his works had, then, been part of the cultural landscape for me and my contemporaries at York. We came mostly from the urban middle-classes, where any notion of the middle-*brow* was either simply foreign (the term certainly played no part in discourse during our student years) or was converted into implicitly class-based forms of snobbish put-down, sometimes disguised as style criticism. An inadvertent example might have been Peggy Mellers's (Wilfrid's then wife) humorous response to my enthusiasm for the César Franck String Quintet that we had just heard in a Lyons Concert Hall event: "Oh you'll grow out of it, my dear."

Wilfrid's approach to the course, and how he delivered his key parts of it, was generally to dispense with style-, age- or class-based distinctions of 'taste' (however much he may have embraced them in his *Scrutiny* days, as a member of the circle around F. R. Leavis). When lecturing on what he was still prepared to number amongst the 'great' works of the old Great Tradition, it was always clear that the mythic status of that tradition might be threatened as much as celebrated by his eclectically wide-ranging enthusiasms. These crossed boundaries not only of 'brow', but also of nations, cultures and continents. Anything that moved, excited, or even just amused him was presented to us as worthy of understanding and sympathy – as potentially communicating something about human values that was worth saying. It could be Bach or Bessie Smith, Beethoven or The Beatles, Couperin or Satie or John Cage. While he never, as I recall, 'taught' us any of the Britten works in the way that he taught us the Bach B minor Mass or Debussy's *Pelléas et Melisande*, we knew that he wrote and cared deeply about them. In a never-repeated (disapproved of by the Aldeburgh elite?) posthumous discussion programme about Britten on BBC Radio, chaired by Paul Griffiths (in 1980 or '81, I think), the question of Britten's sexuality had been boldly raised, and Wilfrid, no less boldly, had responded with words (I recall them imperfectly) to the effect: "Well, I'm a *very* heterosexual sort of chap [pause for an audible chuckle], but Britten's music still speaks to me of profoundly human troubles and concerns and moves me accordingly."

One other Britten work that very specifically moved *me* in my undergraduate years played no part in our course, although I had eagerly watched the first TV showing of the BBC's remarkable filmed production of *Billy Budd* in December 1966. Living, as my family still did, in the London suburbs, I was used to keeping in touch with concert and opera events in the capital when I was at home, and at the end of our second year, in the summer of 1968 – fired perhaps by memories of *Peter Grimes* the previous year – I noticed that *Billy Budd* was being revived at Covent Garden, in its still newish two-act form. It was presented – as I now realize – with "stripped and simplified"[2] versions of the original sets of John Piper, with their wonderfully swirling, marbled-effect backdrops behind and above an impressively realistic, sideways-on version of *The Indomitable*. What I recall certainly looked more or less like the first production as illustrated in the *Cambridge Opera Handbook* on *Billy Budd* by Mervyn Cooke and Philip Reed.[3] They duly mention the production I saw as having been launched in 1964, but fail to register its revival in 1968. I was present at the second of just three performances, conducted magnificently by Georg Solti and with Richard Lewis as Captain Vere.

How lucky, once again, I was. The fabled all-male opera hit me full on – partly, perhaps, because it was the year after the partial decriminalization of homosexuality, but I was excited by the richness and colour of the wonderfully lit production, and no less by the music. The greyly drifting bitonal mist of the Prologue's opening (suggesting a calm, unfriendly sea glimpsed through the parting clouds of Vere's memory) and the harshly naturalistic, dissonantly piping on-deck whistles of the busy opening of Scene 1 seemed to provide a perfect foil for the "dragging" B minor work-song of the sailor chorus, holystoning the deck as an oppressed 'mass' controlled by the First Mate's whip.

Chowrimootoo spares us his reading of this as, no doubt, a reversion from fake modernism to 'sentimentality'. Then (as now) I found myself profoundly impressed by the boldness of the unashamed range of expressive means by which Britten articulates the drama musically, once again foregrounding the chorus as a collective 'character' in the drama.

For example: the opera performs a peculiarly powerful, quasi-cinematic move when, at the end of Act I, Scene 2, Vere (with *The Indomitable* now entering enemy waters) is left alone in his cabin, reading Plutarch. Below deck, off-duty members of the crew can be heard singing a kind of shanty before sleeping – here quite deliberately and appropriately a 'sentimental' song about journeying and parting, the kind of song that has ever brought comfort at nightfall in such circumstances. It is important to register precisely what happens. We know that Vere has been moved by the singing; he had said as much to the first lieutenant and the sailing master. Now alone, he "lays his book down and listens to the singing between decks." The curtain falls for the scene change, facilitated by an orchestral interlude in which we seem to meditate with him on the melody of the song and the thoughts that it might awaken. This establishes what film theorists might call a 'suturing' link between us and Vere as listeners. We hear it, as it were, through his sympathetic and emotionally engaged ears. When the curtain rises again, we see the whole of the berth deck, in a kind of grandiose 'panning shot'; we are confronted also by a great body of male voices singing, 'broadly' and at full volume the song of farewell: "Blow her away, blow her to Hilo. . . . Say farewell, say farewell." It should indeed blow *us* away – a glorious moment of visceral musical and emotional power, in which the full burden and significance of Vere's sympathy is borne in upon us.[4]

It is, of course, our sympathy, as much as Vere's, that is now awakened for the full-voiced oppressed men – in many cases, indeed, '*im*-pressed' in the old naval sense. Billy Budd and his two fellow sailors had themselves been forcibly (if legally) 'recruited' from *The Rights o'Man*, their former vessel. Billy's injudiciously fond farewell to his former ship utilizes the melody of *The Indomitable's* holy-stoning crew: "Farewell to you forever. . . . Farewell old *Rights o'Man*." He will recall and perhaps grasp the deeper significance of that potently symbolic farewell, then so nearly misunderstood on *The Indomitable*, when facing his death at the end of Act II, Scene 3. He has been visited by the chaplain and heard his story of "the good boy hung and gone to glory for the likes of me." Vere's inadvertent, but poignantly significant, adoption of Billy's subsequent words in his own Epilogue ("But I've sighted a sail in the storm, the far-shining sail . . .") accompanies his recollection of the ill-fated boy's cry of "Starry Vere, God bless you!" before he was hanged from the yard-arm above them. It reinforces our sense that the 'innocence' threatened by 'guilt', in this manifestation of that underlying preoccupation of Britten's sought-for morality, is mirrored in *Vere's* confrontation with the guilt of Claggart, whom Billy had involuntarily struck dead when tongue-tied by the lies of the Master at Arms's accusation. This had seemed shockingly to nullify or simply bypass Billy's earlier naively expressed love for Vere, and desire to serve him. The opera is of course as much about Claggart and Vere as it is about Billy. *His* fundamentally uncomplicated goodness is, nevertheless, the tragic fulcrum and incitement of the deadly balance between the Captain and his Master at Arms.

The broad structure can of course be grasped by reading the libretto. But it was what this, like other successful operas, offers *in the process* of dramatically articulating its 'message' that was sending me back to opera houses in my spare time: ascending to high amphitheatres and balconies by what were then still segregated and uncarpeted stairs from side entrances, out of sight of the wealthy highbrows' loggias and crush bars.[5] Purposefully skirting the sociologists and psychologists of culture, and the 'brow' police, I sought the gloriously messy, mixed-brow, mixed-style rewards of Wagnerian and post-Wagnerian opera, German, Italian or even, in this case, British. Like other denizens of 'the gods', I was paying precisely for the fallen, 'brow'-*beating*, emotional and, yes, 'sentimental' pleasures of the magic theatre. Here the desecrating "gaslights of . . . the most rococo and degraded of all forms of art"[6] that so horrified William Morris in relation to Wagner's staging of the German myths appeared redeemed by the great choral moments, the show-stopping arias, the grand scenic effects and the engulfing orchestral overtures and interludes. They invited and incited emotional experiences that felt closer to mass-culture cinema than the audience-improving austerities and overplayed ideological awareness of the 'director's operas' to come. The inventively worthy, illusion-busting features of those productions can too easily mute or even silence the no-less-complex ideological implications and aspirations of originally conceived staging, with its 'spectacle' and encouragement to 'identification', derived from shockingly popular genres like the 'gothic melodrama' whose presence in *The Turn of the Screw* is squeamishly identified by Chowrimootoo.[7]

Perhaps such things still cannot really be said in serious musicological company, which is why they highlight and help to explain the prolonged problematic status of opera in musical scholarship, and the once transgressive quality (and consequent self-consciousness) of pioneering Verdi studies in the 1950s and '60s. One such scholar, Joseph Kerman (anxious to reinforce his fundamentally highbrow intentions and affiliations), made sure to list the failings of the more reprehensibly popular Puccini in his *Opera as Drama* (1956 and subsequent revisions), where Berg's *Wozzeck* – that gift to modernist anti-opera opera-scholars – merits ten pages to the single paragraph devoted to *Peter Grimes*. Such observations could not have been made with impunity in the York Music Department in the early 1970s, where I perhaps ill-advisedly stayed to write my doctoral thesis on Mahler. By then the new compositional austerities and technological-'experimental' eccentricities of what might be called 'political' modernism held sway. Even Wilfrid Mellers's eclectic openness seemed almost deliberately to marginalize (and popularize) itself as he concentrated on The Beatles and tried to persuade himself that the experimental circus he had set in motion was really as much fun as it sometimes wasn't. But it often could be, in all honesty, and York remained a highly stimulating place to be, if only, on occasion, to pull the leg of a dedicated Stockhausen fanatic or to suggest to one experimentalist composer that climbing lamp posts in order to empty bags of flour over elderly ladies in Harrogate might not be as beneficial to their health and well-being as it might arguably have been to their political self-awareness. As I have already observed, although two of the most widely performed mid-twentieth-century composers (meaning Britten and Shostakovich) visited the department (Britten no more, I think, after 1969, and Shostakovich once in 1972, just after I had left[8]), they were no longer admitted to the realms of 'relevance' by Boulezian hard-liners, for all that they might have found common ground with Britten in his aversion to *Der Rosenkavalier*.

I too, in fact, lost some of my enthusiasm for Britten in that context. My newly awakened interest *in* Richard Strauss, along with Wagner, had a greater bearing on my central preoccupation with Mahler. But it was Mahler who rather unexpectedly drew me a little closer to the Aldeburgh 'set', even as I became dissatisfied with some of Britten's newest offerings. His 'TV opera' *Owen Wingrave* was one of these, although I was clearly still sufficiently committed to the cause to have bought a copy of the hastily published libretto and read it in advance of its first broadcast on BBC2 on 16th May 1971. As I had no television of my own in my graduate garret, close to the York football ground, I had welcomed the invitation to view it in the house of some friends who lived a short walk away.

I had at that time begun to keep a diary, and on returning to my garret that Sunday evening, I recorded my impressions of what has, in truth, never been one of my favourite Britten operas:

> It would, I think, have been disappointing if I had not read the libretto beforehand. As it was: pretty much as I had expected. I still feel the second act to 'be' the opera – and certainly here it was that the real 'music' came.

Examining my diary now, I note that not much more than a month earlier, Stravinsky had died, and I had been moved by his passing, for all that his later works did not much interest me. The *Symphony of Psalms* was of course one of the works we had performed at school and that I had enjoyed and have continued to hold in high regard. Most of the supposedly 'neo-classical' works bored me in comparison with the glittering magic of *The Firebird*, of *Petrushka*, even the violence and desolation of *The Rite of Spring*. But with him had gone that living connection with the world of Tchaikovsky, Debussy and, indeed Mahler, all three of whom Stravinsky had seen and heard in the course of his long and eventful life.

Much at that time seemed to me a touch life-*less*, dull and somehow 'after-the-event' by comparison with the world that resounded and was confronted in Mahler, with whom my attention was engaged full-time as I worked my way through the then rather short library shelf of books on him in English. After making the most of Alma's *Gustav Mahler: Memories and Letters*, I was grinding my way laboriously through her still untranslated edition of the *Briefe*, dictionary to hand – my German improving slowly as I uncovered what seemed to be treasures on every page, as no less in the similarly untranslated *Erinnerungen* of Natalie Bauer-Lechner.

I was then also in the process of discovering that Wilfrid Mellers was in truth not terribly interested in what I was trying to do, or in offering the sort of supervision that I needed (I was still too over-awed by him, and too fond to challenge or criticize). During my first graduate year I sought David Blake's advice, and he had taken me on, promising to smooth the path of my embarrassed but necessary defection. I was very grateful for that, as indeed for his efforts to help: above all, to *read* what I was writing (at far too great a length). I am sure it was with his acquiescence that I had rather nervously made contact with Donald Mitchell, the most recent editor of Alma's famous memoir. I had, I think, little clear knowledge at that time of the role Mitchell played in Britten's later life, nor of what strange corridors and distant doors into the world of Aldeburgh his generous offer to meet and talk to me in London would later open. But that was all to come after I had in fact made my first visit to Aldeburgh during the festival, and even performed with the York Chamber Choir in the Jubilee Hall, in that very June of 1971.

Notes

1 In recent years, substantial new additions have extended the department's facilities.
2 Mervyn Cooke and Philip Reed, *Cambridge Opera Handbooks, Benjamin Britten 'Billy Budd'* (Cambridge: Cambridge University Press, 1993), 140, quoting Andrew Porter.
3 Ibid., 80.
4 I will return later to Harper-Scott's very different reading of Vere's character.
5 This was still the case in the 1970s at both the Royal Opera House and English National Opera at the Coliseum.
6 This from a letter Morris sent to the brother of Alfred Forman, who had sent Morris the latter's translation of Wagner's text of *Die Walküre*. Quoted from Mackail's 1899 biography of Morris by Andrew Heywood in 'William Morris and Music. Craftsman's Art?' in *The Musical Times*, Autumn 1998, Vol. 1, 1864, 34.
7 I allude here not least to Brecht, whose satirical rejection of the music of popular cinema ("one of the most blossoming branches of the international narcotics traffic") was summed up in his 1935 essay 'On the Use of Music in the Epic Theatre', which I further discuss in Peter Franklin, *Seeing*

Through Music. Gender and Modernism in Classic Hollywood Film Scores (Oxford and New York: Oxford University Press, 2011), 44–6.
8 Shostakovich's visit was almost certainly thanks to the Department's excellent resident Fitzwilliam Quartet, which had devoted itself to his quartets; they were among the earliest to perform and record his Fifteenth String Quartet.

5 Singing at Aldeburgh: Musical Scholarship

That Aldeburgh trip must have been distantly linked to the Britten-Pears York visit in 1967, when Peter Aston was already turning the departmental Chamber Choir into a viable entity. It would soon be able to tackle the *Hymn to St Cecilia* and *Rejoice in the Lamb*, and to give public performances in and around York. Aston may have sought to capitalize on Britten's memory of their earlier visit when writing to him about the choir and suggesting, presumably in 1970, that he could possibly bring it to Aldeburgh (a few years and some further visits later, he left York for the department at East Anglia, where his relationship with Aldeburgh became stronger).

I remain enormously grateful to him for the experience I had of singing in that choir, through to the end of the 1970–1 academic year, the second of my three state-funded years as a graduate student. My diary certainly testifies to reawakened Britten-enthusiasm in the run-up to our two-night stay at the Thorpeness Country Club in June 1971. We arrived in the late afternoon after a long coach ride from York. It had given me my first glimpse of Cambridge and had finally brought us down along the seafront and through Aldeburgh itself. Our spirits were high – in my case significantly raised by the presence of at least two of my temporarily returned undergraduate contemporaries, at a time when I was sinking into the well-known gloom of graduate isolation and depression. For me that Aldeburgh trip inspired a kind of regression to an earlier, lighter self: the sixth-form Britten and Mahler devotee who never entirely expected to succeed in gaining a university place at all, let alone one that might bring him into direct contact with the composer of *War Requiem* and *Peter Grimes*.

My 1971 diary includes an extended and excited account of that visit to the Aldeburgh Festival, reminding me that while there had been the usual student gravitation towards finding a pub after our supper on the first evening, a few of us chose instead to walk along the shingle bar back into Aldeburgh, to absorb the atmosphere:

> The excitement of actually being in Aldeburgh, walking by the fishing boats etc., seeing the Moot Hall, thinking of *Grimes* – everything seemed

peculiarly good. . . . Also lots of birds – and the sea, high and always audible, washing against the shingle.

The following morning, after a good breakfast, we had been loaded back onto our coach and driven into Aldeburgh for a short rehearsal in the Jubilee Hall before our 11.00 am concert. My diary attributes the clear awareness that it was all truly 'happening' to the moment when

> Peter Pears walked in for a few minutes. To this excitement was added the next: of suddenly finding Imogen Holst wishing us well in the dressing-room behind the stage before we went on.

A few of us, nerves tensing, had taken a little walk between the rehearsal and the start of the concert; we were feeling apprehensive:

> The concert itself was introduced by Pears (good audience, the Jubilee Hall almost full), who said nice things about York, as well as thanking us, as we had "suggested ourselves that we might come", which rather put the matter in a nutshell, but was clearly well meant. Apart from nerves in the Hacomplaynt, we sang fairly well.[1] Applause was good, and in general the audience seemed very well disposed toward us (including Pears and a beaming Imogen Holst sitting up in the gallery at the side).
>
> Greater delights were to follow (Peter Aston was deservedly very pleased about it all): lunch was laid in the open, under awnings at the back of the hall and only a stone's throw from the sea. To this we were conducted by Pears and Imogen Holst, each of whom took a seat at the head of one of the two tables. There was a splendid salad, wine, hot sweets, coffee – but how kind of Pears and I. H. to act as host and hostess! I must confess I had wondered even if he would come to the concert. He gave apologies for "Ben Britten" who would "certainly have come had he not been rehearsing" etc. And then the compliments. Imogen Holst was verging on the ecstatic: "Such wonderful music and performed *right*! My father used to do the Byrd at Morely College but they couldn't sing; all the things he used to try to do, you *did*! Hacomplaynt is my favourite composer (!).[2] I have never enjoyed anything so much . . ."

We were due to leave on our coach more or less straight after lunch, and Imogen Holst had apologized for needing to rush off to another rehearsal. Before she left, however, she had got wind of our desire to see the Maltings at Snape. Supported by Pears, she won Peter Aston's support for a ten-minute stopover there on the way back, and before long, we were indeed glimpsing the dark sloping roof of the Maltings, where we duly disembarked, to find Peter Pears already waiting for us and ready to give us a quick tour. He led us through the Sidney Nolan exhibition and into the hall, where he had the lights turned on so that we could see it properly. Duly impressed and deeply grateful, we were soon back on our bus and heading to Colchester, where we were to repeat the concert – the arrangement having made by another of my year group, in fact the very same friend with whom I had gone to see *Peter Grimes* in 1967 (he was living and now teaching in Colchester).

* * *

Having grown up, passed through school and entered university in a time when homosexuality was technically against the law, I was alert to the 1967 move to lessen the legal constraints. I was no less familiar with the continuing difficulty of 'being' gay, as an undergraduate (at the time apparently the only one of my year group in Music). It was a period before relevant student support and social organizations were available. Only during the latter part of my graduate time at York did the situation begin to change – precisely when my own growing disaffection with the Music Department's compositional 'experimentalism' and performance-based preoccupations confirmed my sense of becoming a somewhat conservative-seeming recluse.

My engagement with Mahler's intense and complex expressive world, and how it related to the social and cultural circumstances of his time, felt more truly alive and relevant to whatever the future might hold for me. At that time the relative openness of Britten and Pears, living together, performing together and riding the 'open secret' right into the support and affection of the Royal Family, added greatly to the attractive lustre of their world, in which 'highbrow' seriousness and intensity was matched in a seemingly exemplary way by the unconventional sincerity (as I hoped and imagined) of their relationship and lifestyle. They had become, as we might now say, 'role models'. I paid the price and also reaped some of the benefits in those times. My periodic re-engagement with the communicative power of still relevant-seeming Britten works confirmed their character for me as so many messages in bottles that I seemed to know how to read.

It was in relation to all this that early rumours of Britten's final operatic project struck me and some of my friends uncomfortably as perhaps a step too far. The choice of Mann's *Death in Venice* (already complicatedly related to my doctoral project) sounded like the injudicious courting of some kind of aesthetic disaster. In the summer of 1971 that was still some way off in the future (it was premiered in 1973); it was, however, later that summer when I finally resolved to contact Donald Mitchell, to introduce myself and to see if I might seek his specific advice and assistance on certain detailed matters arising from my research. He was, after all, the leading British Mahler scholar of the day and was well connected with other continental and American workers in the field.

Limiting my proposed topics of conversation to questions about Mahler's part in the piano arrangement of Bruckner's Third Symphony and the chronology of the early *Wunderhorn* songs, my letter evidently impressed him as serious, and bore fruit in a meeting in London on the 19th October 1971. I caught an early train down from York and met him that morning, at what might have been the main Faber & Faber headquarters (before Faber Music was fully established). Wherever it was, it struck me as being rather disappointingly housed in a London terrace, the building reminding me of the informal, 'domestic' atmosphere of the old York Music Department in Micklegate. But I was with him for the better part of an hour, and he was charmingly amiable and friendly. He seemed younger than I had expected, wearing a dark pin-striped suit and coming over rather effectively as the smooth but approachable 'executive'. I found him out on one or two things (he had not compared the texts of the Mahler *Wunderhorn* songs with their originals in Arnim and Brentano), but he had certainly amassed a mountain of factual material and was happy to talk – not least about his plans to revise his *Gustav Mahler: The Early Years*, with which I was of course familiar. And then there was his current work on a 'next' volume (this would be *Gustav Mahler: The Wunderhorn Years*, published in 1975). He also talked about plans to publish Deryck Cooke's performing version of the Tenth Symphony draft. Only at one point did he allude to Britten, when talking about composers and how they came by the texts they set, mentioning his own "experience with composers."

The meeting marked the beginning of a long period of cautious, on my part rather awed, friendship with Mitchell, whose interest really shone a light into the dark corners of my hitherto rather isolated quest to understand Mahler in York, with no real scholarly support and little obvious interest (David Blake's aside) on the part of others in what I was doing. Mitchell was to play a significant role in helping me to manoeuvre myself onto a viable career path in musicology.

Opera in the '70s and *Death in Venice*

Here is Chowrimootoo on opera in Britain at that time:

> As scholars have often observed, the twentieth century was a troubled time for opera; when not being denounced as a bastion of elitism, it was charged with prefiguring "some of the worst abominations" of the culture-industry. Yet even so, the late 1960s and early 1970s represented the real low point.[3]

Having been around in that period, I am bound to suggest that it depends which scholars you read and who they were writing for. I confess that I recall it as a peculiarly rich and lively period in my own consumption of opera, let alone in the staging of recent or new works. The BBC played its part for Britten with its 1966 *Billy Budd*, followed by the no-less-famous *Peter Grimes* in 1969 and *Owen Wingrave* in 1971. Following the eruptive intervention at the 1968 Aldeburgh Festival of Birtwistle's *Punch and Judy*, London in the early 1970s saw not only the premiere of Britten's *Death in Venice* (1973) but, before that, Tippett's *The Knot Garden* in December 1970 and Peter Maxwell Davies's *Taverner* in 1972 (both at Covent Garden). All of the last three chanced to be by non-heterosexual composers, and Tippett's was one of the first to introduce recognizably 'gay' characters onto the operatic stage. But of course a great many other operas, apart from those new and British, were being consumed in Chowrimootoo's supposedly 'low point' years of the late 1960s and early '70s. These were the glory days of Sadlers Wells turning into English National Opera at the Coliseum on St Martin's Lane. More specifically, it was the era of their great Wagner *Ring* operas in English, which were introduced with premieres in the following order:

1970   *The Valkyrie*
1971   *The Twilight of the Gods*
1972   *Rhinegold*
1973   *Siegfried*

Nineteen seventy-three saw the first complete ENO *Ring* cycle, selling out to audiences already schooled on Solti's first complete modern recording of the cycle for Decca. I still cherish those records in their big, burnished-looking box that included Deryck Cooke's guide to the cycle and its musical 'motifs'. Chowrimootoo's reference to Arthur Jacobs, in 1969, echoing Adorno's notion that the long-playing record forced "concentration on the music as the true object of opera"[4] can only encourage me to throw, for once, an anti-Adornian spanner into the works and point out that the great asset of the old LP *Ring* cycle was that each opera came with a full-format libretto and translation that allowed one to follow the operas not only with the text but also *the original stage directions*, giving rise to detailed mental images of the kind of stage pictures that were intended to contextualize Wagner's often highly visually orientated music. Perhaps, no *surely*, other denizens of the Coliseum Amphitheatre would have got to know their Wagner in the same way, which might help explain why (both for the initiated and the uninitiated) the curtain rising on the second act of *The Valkyrie* in those days would unfailingly occasion spontaneous applause. It was not just that Ralph Koltai's *Star Trek* set, with its moon landscape and huge shiny spheres looking like congealed mercury, was thrillingly up-to-the-minute, but it was also a 'neutral' mythical space in the sense that it imposed no obvious ideological or historical 'reading' and easily accommodated any novice Wagnerian's pre-imagined version of the required 'Wild and Rocky Pass'.

Death in Venice, too, was linked to contemporary visual media experience and most specifically the cinematic. For all that subsequently emerged about Britten being advised by his lawyers not to watch Visconti's version (he had in fact been scathing about "a few deplorable photographs" of it he had seen in April 1971, the year of its release[5]), the already-celebrated film based on Mann's novella rather conveniently played its part in arousing the appetite of the expanding popular metropolitan opera audience for Britten's version, which premiered at Aldeburgh in June 1973. The supposedly "minimalist aesthetic"[6] of John Piper's sets for the opera, whose three-sided scenic towers moved and turned to facilitate the kind of rapid, 'cinematic' scene changes that Britten had first pioneered in *The Turn of the Screw*, were in truth more scenic and colourful than some contemporary critics suggested, and black-background 'action' scenes were supplied with music whose frequently 'scenic' qualities allowed audiences to imagine Visconti's Venice while hearing Britten. This is relevant to Chowrimootoo's intricately complex worrying about the opera and the taste boundaries it appeared both to respect and transgress. His best reading of Piper's and Britten's intention is that they were aiming to set the erotic against the ideal, to "stage the body in order to dematerialize it . . . to highlight the ideal by foregrounding the real."[7]

In due course I will record my own recollection of the staging and impact of Britten's last opera – which I had made a conscious decision to pay serious attention to. Surely I was duty-bound to study carefully this new opera by a contemporary composer for whom I had great admiration and affection; and I had obvious personal reasons for wondering how Britten might be going to confront the 'open secret' of his own sexuality in relation to what I had initially believed to be a disastrous choice of subject matter. Those reasons seem, in retrospect, closely bound up with the cultural mechanism of the open secret and its maintenance, which Philip Brett would address in his fine essay 'Britten's Dream' that first appeared in Ruth Solie's 1993 collection *Musicology and Difference: Gender and Sexuality in Music Scholarship* and was subsequently reprinted in George Haggerty's edition of Brett's *Music and Sexuality in Britten: Selected Essays* (2006).[8]

Nineteen seventy-three was a difficult year, not least in my own life. I had left York and was back living with my parents and sister in Hatch End, where the family had moved around the time I left school. I still had work to do on my thesis and was busily applying for university jobs, getting interviews for three or four that summer, but without any success. With little or no money to my name, my parents were initially supporting me. They quite rightly gave me to understand that I would soon need to pay my way. I was left with little option other than to sign on as formally 'unemployed' in order at least to receive the dole. But it was a sufficiently humiliating business to persuade me to apply for graduate entry into the Civil Service. I was interviewed and accepted. By October I was working in the Home Office as an executive officer in the Criminal Injuries Compensation Board and really rather enjoying being a conventional 9–5 worker, commuting into London each day on the Metropolitan Line, tending my case files with a pleasant group of people, mostly of my own age, and bringing in money at last. Some of it went to my mother for upkeep, a small amount was saved and more than a little went on opera trips in that politically tense and troubled period.

In the previous January, Ted Heath had succeeded in taking the country into the EU (the 'Common Market'), but thereafter things had gone seriously wrong. The Irish situation was violently dreadful, unemployment was high and miners' strikes, leading to power cuts, were taking us towards the 'three-day week' that would ultimately end Heath's premiership and bring Harold Wilson back as prime minister for a short period. Things were little better in the wider world, and that October saw the outbreak of the Arab-Israeli 'Yom Kippur' war, leading to fears of a widening and possibly nuclear conflict, precisely at the time of two memorable trips I made to see Britten operas.

It seems extraordinary to me now to record that on the 15th October, I took an old university friend to the Sadlers Wells theatre to see one of the English Opera Group's two revival performances of *The Turn of the Screw* – the very first opera I had ever seen, in that same theatre, long ago (as it already seemed). On this occasion Peter Pears himself took the role of Quint and sang the Prologue, incredibly just three days before *Death in Venice* was to open at Covent Garden for the first time. Jill Gomez was the Governess, Colin Graham the producer and Kenneth Montgomery conducted (scenery and costumes, of which I have no specific recollection, were by Yolanda Sonnabend). I recorded the event in my diary:

> A beautiful production. . . . It's a fine piece, wonderfully worked as a whole – a little bald in places perhaps, but the moments are there (the spine-chilling 'sextet' of Act I, when the two children become the fragile, quivering focus of all the forces of both light and darkness that are at play).

However, the main operatic event of the month was indeed to be *Death in Venice*. Booking for one of the three initial performances at Covent Garden was a task I had managed in good time, securing two tickets for what was in fact the last of the three, on Wednesday, 24th October. My record of that event suggests that I might have heard the opera before seeing it. I can find no evidence of having done so, but the second of Edward Greenfield's critical essays on it, an extended extract from which is reproduced in Volume Six of the *Letters from a Life*, records that by 7th July he had heard the opera half a dozen times "thanks to radio, tape and dress rehearsal."[9] Had I too heard a radio broadcast of it? I had certainly furnished myself with the libretto, which my copy tells me I had acquired in "August 1973." I read it carefully, but what mattered, of course, was seeing it in the theatre, 'being there'. My diligence over securing tickets was additionally rewarded in an unexpected way, as my late-evening, rather breathless diary account, begun on the 24th October, reveals (the unbracketed rhetorical dots do not indicate omissions):

Wednesday 24 October 73

> . . . this evening, a great occasion. Britten's *Death in Venice* at Covent Garden. Perhaps it is as well that I and my pen must soon sleep, since

I still feel very 'full' about it all . . . the first time I have given voice in public for a good while. But after such a piece, with such a performance by Pears (who, astonishingly, *looked* like a middle-aged Thomas Mann at the start – with wig and moustache) . . . and then at the end. . . . I had hardly dared hope. Suddenly amidst the applause I realized that a spotlight was picking out a box on the other side of the theatre from where we were sitting. It was Britten himself – smiling at the stage, looking almost hurt by the light . . . people all around suddenly noticing and realizing. And then all on stage turned up to him. For a moment he stood . . . bowed, old, with a walking stick. He smiled and briefly acknowledged the applause. Donald Mitchell was in attendance behind him – quickly taking his arm and leading him back, out of the box and the light with the many eyes turned upon him. It was a most moving triumph. And it was a triumph. A great sense of togetherness, of expectation and satisfaction, of being profoundly *with* and *for* this man. . . . Oh of course, there were the titters in the foyer, a certain element in the audience etc. . . . But that music . . . the yearning serenity of the closing bars, the final moment of vision (almost?) . . . It was an occasion . . . occasioning hope. A brave and beautiful piece.

Thursday 25 October 73

It would seem that we teetered on the brink for a time today. As usual I have wilfully tried to avoid all news bulletins, papers etc., but one could somehow *feel* it – as if the human psyche were indeed one vast, collective unit. A single headline was unavoidable as I got to Euston Square this evening: "Russia goes in!" (followed by something about "nuclear alert") . . . and in that single exclamation-mark was embodied all the panic and the excitement – the gleam of the death wish.

And so I am brought back to *Death in Venice*. The light of day has if anything only led me to enlarge upon and confirm my excitement of yesterday. One must tread so carefully . . . in finding a suitable way of confessing that here was a *great* theatrical experience of our time – and I use such a broad term as 'theatrical' with serious intent. But I have been haunted not least by the *music* itself and feel certain now that the work is everything, and more, that one could have hoped for. Already I begin to feel at home in its world . . . the subtle use of the motives, the often brief, all-too-short, but quite exquisite melodic spans that flower in the part of Aschenbach against the often austere orchestral or piano accompaniment (a touch of ice . . . of crystalline glitter . . .). But the experience as a totality remains, and increasingly, precious in the memory.

The still centre of the entire work, the dramatic nexus close to the end, has obsessed me throughout the day. It is that passage where, having eaten the musty strawberries (that haunting siren-call of the strawberry girl!) Aschenbach sinks into a kind of total dejection, a profound comprehension of the state into which he has caused himself to fall – the utter pity of it all.

It is that passage where, crumpled in an untidy heap against the fountain in the deserted square Pears/Aschenbach (how can one distinguish between the two?) recites very gently to himself lines recollected from Plato. . . . "Does beauty lead to wisdom, Phaedrus?" Pears sang this as if he really were the last man left alive, at the edge of a vast sea. Gentle, *pianissimo* beyond imagining – the music itself exquisite . . . calling to mind that phrase from the *War Requiem*: 'Was it for this the clay grew tall? (or, still further back, Mahler – the *Kindertotenlieder*. . . or '*aus tiefem Traum . . . doch alle Lust . . .* ').

And then, and then suddenly I would write it all out: the clanging, swinging and swaying 'Venice' music of the Overture (with John Piper's fine back-projected image of St Marks, gradually growing richer and brighter) – or that moment when, before the final scene of Act I, the scenery towers slide back to the wings (white facing only now); the black curtain rises to reveal the projection screen blank, blinding white (lit from behind) – "Here will I stay. . . ." The stage becomes vast and empty about Pears-Aschenbach – brilliant in sunlight – and he turns, alone, and walks slowly, silhouetted against the back-lit whiteness, into the sun, his arms held just out from the sides of his body, almost in supplication . . .

Yes, let's have hope . . . all is not lost. I think the memory of that performance will live with me for a long time to come – the memory of the boy (powdered white to appear somewhat cherubic, abstracted a little, but rather beautiful), moving in posed gestures away into the far back left corner of the stage (Aschenbach lying dead, front right, his head turned towards him), the music turning suddenly toward the close of Mahler's Tenth; and Britten himself – ill, so old in the plush box, somehow so small in the huge ornate theatre, but the centre of it all – *fons et origo* – the individual at the heart of all the external realities that made up the production.

> "And now, Phaedrus, I will go.
> But you stay here
> and when your eyes no longer see me,
> then you go too."

* * *

These recollections from 1973, half a century ago, have perhaps no greater claim upon authority, or unmediated 'authenticity', than do the assessments of the critics cited by Chowrimootoo, who would have firm grounds for diagnosing my own recollections as marked by 'sentimentality'. This I can live with, if I am permitted to own that term as meaning 'filled with *sentiment*'. It was undoubtedly an emotional experience that I have recalled, along with aspects of the staging to which in fact none of the accounts Chowrimootoo quotes seem to do full justice. But where his own term "visceral" carries connotations of unseemly excess, of "the 'cheap' pleasures of popular fiction,"[10]

I find myself entirely in agreement with his own partial step back from fretting about the opera's *feigning* of some sort of idealistic modernism (it "wears its formalism on its sleeve, right from the opening pages"[11]). We know the sort of thing that earnest analysts could get their teeth into, serial processes and all. As a consequence, I also support his admission, albeit oddly backhanded, that the "tendency to focus on questions of long-term structure while blocking one's ears to . . . immediate visceral dimensions" can fail to do justice to the musical experience.[12]

His assertion, as I read it, is that some of the ostensibly more favourable critical responses to the opera were in fact trying to maintain the above-mentioned tendency: to hold on to its outward signs of 'advanced' or 'modernist' techniques of pitch organization and textural austerity in the spirit of what he calls "sublimation" (we might understand that as attempting to gild a fake lily). The implication is that they were aspiring to some kind of idealistic, 'intellectual' reading of the opera to which (let us be frank) its lapses into tonal self- and audience-indulgence seem rather significantly to give the lie.

My perplexed reaction to this hangs in part upon the absence of any really nuanced critical account of the source Thomas Mann novella, itself engaged in large measure in a self-ironizing game of mocking and progressively undermining Aschenbach's persistent tendency to engage precisely *in sublimation* – the very kind of sublimation Chowrimootoo rather cattily analyses in the hoodwinked critics he seeks to put right, playing, as it were, the Serenus Zeitblom to Britten's and Myfanwy Piper's perhaps rather better understanding of Leverkühn-Aschenbach's[13] thematized evasions, as a celebrated writer, in the name of aesthetic propriety. His life, Mann tells us, had been one

> of self-conquest, a life against odds, dour, steadfast, abstinent; he had made it symbolical of the kind of over-strained heroism the time admired, and he was entitled to call it manly, even courageous.
>
> Thus did the fond man's folly condition his thoughts; thus did he seek to hold his dignity upright in his own eyes.[14]

Mann's mapping of Aschenbach's decline complicatedly, if characteristically, structured the autobiographical aspect of his own story – written *in* Venice (in 1911), inspired by a real Tadzio – in which the fictional writer is given the facial characteristics of Gustav Mahler. Mann had observed the latter at the rehearsal and first performance of the composer's vast Eighth Symphony in Munich the previous autumn, the last premiere of Mahler's career. By choosing that link between his literary central character and a practitioner of *music*, Mann's overriding artistic purpose seems to have been to produce a cautionary tale, not about "cheap thrills" but about 'Art' itself: of its very nature open to 'highbrow' evasion of a different, more troubling kind of truth. To suggest that Britten understood this is to read his opera as the reverse of a 'middlebrow' failure to sustain 'high' artistic purpose – what he and Chowrimootoo might agree as being represented by 'Modernism' and its ways here. For this reason I submit that the latter seems intent upon reading it from the anachronistic perspective of a 1970s partisan modernism which Britten was arguably challenging. Like Chowrimootoo, the self-appointed highbrows of their day almost failed to grasp that it might be read as mocking the very modernism that it flirts with, as signalling Aschenbach's own dangerous commitment to 'sublimation', whereas the opera speaks through its (or his) own methods of subterfuge quite deliberately to reveal the kind of 'truth' that Aschenbach refuses to confront until it is probably too late.

I say 'almost' failed, since in a revealing, quietly tagged-on comment at the very end of this final chapter of his book, Chowrimootoo reaches the following conclusion:

> Perhaps the problem with bourgeois operas like *Death in Venice* was not that they revealed supposedly irreconcilable aesthetic categories. It was, rather, that they exposed modernism's own acts of sublimation, laying bare the precariousness of the great divide.[15]

Of course! But why is it a 'problem'? More precisely, to *whom* is it a problem? Chowrimootoo's treatment of *Death in Venice* sets up an approach to the work that entails hearing and viewing it through a dense, at times barely penetrable screen of conflicting views of the work, constructed out of a carefully excavated network of contemporary perspectives whose backgrounds and intentional characteristics seem at times to block any clear, or at least alternative, view of their historical object. A different kind of reception history might have wanted to know more about each critic cited, and about the journals or newspapers for which they wrote; some might have been writing as rather cattily 'knowing' members of the gay community, for whom Britten was as fascinating as he was infuriating – deserving (as it often seemed) of the kind of bullying meted out to someone who didn't quite 'fit' and yet received all the accolades that would have been unavailable to others who did. They were 'cool', as we might now put it, liberated, untroubled by the tensions and repressions that Britten's works often seemed almost to relish and thrive on. But, unlike Britten, they were subsequently unvisited by royal favours or a life peerage.

As I have said, my own experience of Britten's works, specifically here of *Death in Venice*, is probably neither better nor truer than many of those Chowrimootoo utilizes in order to assist him in fending off his own inner "sickly sentimentality" – but so successfully that at times something darker is suddenly glimpsed in a strategy, a turn of phrase that refracts the anger and even viciousness of some of the contemporary critics. This emerges most surprisingly in one of his direct interpretative engagements with the 'visceral' aspect of *Death in Venice*'s gestural manners. It almost pains me to confront it, so far different from mine is his reading of the end of Act I, where the dissonant heterophony of Aschenbach's inner turmoil, following a nearly direct encounter with Tadzio, gives way to that dramatic silence and a cry which resolves onto the quietest and simplest, most vulnerably old-fashioned words, "I love you", sung to the descending major third which is their musical correlate. I well remember, having read the libretto before I heard the opera, wondering how on earth he would set that beautifully simple, dangerously honest final utterance. Aschenbach has finally had to face the reality of Tadzio, hitherto 'sublimated' as an image of eternal perfection, the inspiring embodiment of a beauty that enabled Aschenbach to turn it, and him, into literature, into Art ("what the world waits for"[16]). Now, having been caught up in self-destructive confusion, he is left to voice "the truth at last" (as the stage direction reads), stricken by Tadzio's smile (in the vocal score Aschenbach's last three words are marked "*p* (almost spoken)":[17]

ASCHENBACH ... no one should be smiled at like that!
(then realizing the truth at last)
      I – love you.
(Black out)
END OF ACT I

Here is Chowrimootoo's reading of the underpinning tangle of orchestral lines that crescendo to the point where they break off abruptly, leaving Aschenbach to make his final unaccompanied confession to himself, utilizing the G-sharp to E falling major third. It is supported at the last by horns and double basses gently, if portentously, confirming the E major chord by adding its third and fifth as if from the darkest, albeit pitying depths:

> The sustained bass drone [*sic*], combined with the tenor's "almost spoken" descending third on the words "love you", perfectly captures a sense of post-coital relaxation. . . . Indeed the passage's approximation of orgasm calls to mind the notion of "body music" coined by Daniel Albright.[18]

As if to rub salt into the verbal wound, Chowrimootoo goes on, over the page, to propose that such music might be encouraging the audience to hear it "as ironic or insincere," quoting now a stridently bitchy (or simply homophobic?) review by Conrad Wilson:

> stretches of music seem happy to stay on the level of, say, Puccini and the closing line of Act One has Aschenbach proclaiming "I love you" to the receding figure of the boy, for all the world as if he were Don José singing his flower song to Carmen. Such banalities, however, seem sometimes to be placed deliberately in the score.[19]

Such critical insensitivity was precisely what I might have expected of some of my York contemporaries amongst the composers of 'experimental' or modernist persuasion, before whose dismissive assuredness I might have decided to conceal my rather different response. *That* response might nevertheless have found support from the late and sadly lamented Philip Brett, in his already-cited essay 'Britten's Dream':

> When Aschenbach sings "I love you" at the powerful climax of Act I in his key of E major, there is no avoiding the sense of personal declaration, the importance of which rests entirely in the private sphere – both for the character Aschenbach and by implication for the composer Britten. Such a declaration, it may be thought, would even so have its public effect in robbing the open secret around Britten of its remaining power for his audience. But the way that critical debate grabbed at the straw of allegory offered by the libretto of *Death in Venice* . . . affords a classic instance of the workings of the open secret and, consequently, of the double bind under which the discerning of sexuality in musical drama operates.[20]

Here Brett offers a line on 'sublimation' that Chowrimootoo might have used to pull himself out of the mire of his stickily orgasmic diagnosis (surely to be held in reserve until 'The Dream' in Act II, whose Dionysian climax might more clearly bear the full implication of the *double entendre*).

Notes

1. The works we sang were the Hacomplaynt *Salve Regina*, Tallis's *Lamentations of Jeremiah*, John Paynter's *The Rose*, Peter Aston's *Alleluya Psallat*, Wilfrid Mellers's *Cloud Canticle* and then, after an interval, William Byrd's *Mass for Five Voices*.
2. Only the one composition by him survives.
3. Chowrimootoo, *Middlebrow Modernism*, 150. His own footnote does not reveal the author of the quoted passage, but lists a number of scholars who seem to bear out his general assertion here.
4. Ibid., 151.
5. See Carpenter, *Benjamin Britten*, 518–9.
6. Chowrimootoo, *Middlebrow Modernism*, 153.
7. Ibid., 158.
8. Ruth Solie (ed.), *Musicology and Difference. Gender and Sexuality in Music Scholarship* (Berkeley, Los Angeles and London: University of California Press, 1993), 259–80; Philip Brett, *Music and Sexuality in Britten. Selected Essays*, ed. George E. Haggerty (Berkeley, Los Angeles and London: University of California Press, 2006), 106–28.
9. Philip Reed and Mervyn Cooke (eds.), *Letters from a Life. The Selected Letters of Benjamin Britten, Vol. Six 1966–1976* (Woodbridge: The Boydell Press in association with the Britten-Pears Foundation, 2012), 564.
10. Chowrimootoo, *Middlebrow Modernism*, 148.
11. Ibid., 164–5.

12 Ibid., 168.
13 I refer here to the two central characters of Mann's *Dr Faustus* (1947).
14 Thomas Mann, *Death in Venice*, trans. H.T. Lowe-Porter in *Death in Venice, Tristan, Tonio Kröger* (London: Penguin Books, 1955 etc.), 64.
15 Chowrimootoo, *Middlebrow Modernism*, 175.
16 See Myfanwy Piper, *Death in Venice. An Opera in Two Acts* (London: Faber Music 1973), 21.
17 See Vocal Score (Faber Music), 159.
18 Chowrimootoo, *Middlebrow Modernism*, 167.
19 Ibid., 168.
20 Brett, *Music and Sexuality in Britten*, 125-6.

6 A Trip to East Berlin and the Start of a Career

Fate had evident designs upon me as regards experiences of Britten in the opera house. This was surprisingly borne out by my next encounter with him there. It was on a snowy night the following December, at the *Komische Oper* in East Berlin. I was on the feared but fascinating 'other side' of the notorious Wall that still enclosed the former Allies' sections of Berlin. Retained at the end of the Second World War as part of 'the West', they were now surrounded by what had become the German Democratic Republic (the 'DDR' in German). My presence there was thanks to a bold scheme of David Blake's. My thesis had been completed under his supervision and submitted around the time of my starting work at the Home Office in London. He had floated the idea that he might be able to secure the great East German musicologist Georg Knepler as my External Examiner. David had got to know him while studying in East Berlin with Hanns Eisler as a Mendelssohn Scholar from Cambridge in 1960. He had been planning to visit Knepler that November, and the York administration kindly agreed to my being examined there. This had meant that I had to confess, in a Civil Service training session, that I *would* be visiting the 'other' side of the Iron Curtain ("I can't imagine that any of you will, but I have to ask" had been our trainer's line). As a result I had to attend a special, additional session that involved some 15-minute *film noir* 'frighteners' about entrapment by enemy agents lighting cigarettes on dark corners of rain-swept streets.

Knepler, whom I had previously met on one of his visits to York, was impressive and charming and, as David had warned, took me to task for my ignorance of Marxist approaches to the nineteenth century and the significance of the socialist workers' movement. But he promised not to make me "a scapegoat for the fallacies of Western thought" and proceeded to discuss my work with me in a generous and constructive manner. By the end of the afternoon I had been declared successful and was turned out into the snowy evening, clutching a copy of Christopher Caudwell's *Illusion and Reality* that Knepler had given me as a parting gift. In less than an hour, back in the city centre, I had sorted out how and where to leave my outer garments in the theatre. But the opera had already begun, and I was permitted to do no more

DOI: 10.4324/9781032666631-6

than find a standing-place at the back of the circle in the delightfully ornate old auditorium (encased now in a modern, constructivist concrete block as a result of wartime bombing). I soon began to get my bearings in the first act of Britten's *A Midsummer Night's Dream* – an opera I did not know but was thankful that it was one where my imperfect grasp of German would prove unproblematic.

It had greatly surprised me that they were staging it in East Berlin, but I remember it as a rather beautiful production, with larger-than-life cut-outs of meadow flowers and teasels. The back lighting turned these into a foreground silhouette frieze, as in a Lotte Reiniger animation, through which one glimpsed half-seen fairy figures of the wood moving stealthily. After the interval, in which I had managed to buy a programme, I finally found my excellent reserved seat in the centre of the stalls. My diary entry for the day concluded as follows:

> Apart from Oberon being some species of *baritone* (?!),[1] it was really quite something. The fooling was truly funny, the musical side thoroughly polished – very nice stage effects. And of course it was a work I didn't know! Odd to be hearing it there, of all places, and in German.

The following day found me rising early to make my way out into a still more or less dark winter's morning, across the deserted Alexanderplatz. Above it the eerily lit viewing windows of the *Fernsehturm* (the Television Tower) looked down from the lower part of the large sphere, two thirds of the way up the tapering modernist spire, from which searchlights sent long, slowly swinging beams of silver out into the gloom. Were they warning or watching? I negotiated the journey back to Grünau, to be met by David and Knepler, who proved invaluable in getting me through the airport *Passkontroll*, where it was discovered that I did not have the correct exit visa (only much later did I learn that I should have reported to the police on arrival and got my entry visa stamped with the exit date). While we waited for officialdom to respond to Knepler's senior status as a Party member, he talked a little about his teachers, about Adler, Steuermann and other friends who had been in contact with Schoenberg, like Egon Wellesz.

Eventually we made it back to England, and I returned to my life as a civil servant, periodically submitting myself to unsuccessful interviews for university posts while growing progressively more dissatisfied with my hitherto rather enjoyable life as a real, and yet somehow 'make-believe', London commuter, trying to read while strap-hanging on the Underground and making lunchtime forays into the British Museum from where I worked in Russell Square.

The location was, however, valuable for maintaining my tenuous link with Donald Mitchell. It must have been as a result of the shortened working week during the last crisis of Ted Heath's government (before the General Election that briefly brought Harold Wilson back as prime minister at the beginning of March), that I was able to accept an invitation to meet Donald at Faber's in February. The first appointment was cancelled, as he had to go unexpectedly to Aldeburgh – Britten was still quite ill in the wake of his ill-fated heart operation. On the day in question (Tuesday 5th February 1974), I had sat waiting rather awkwardly in the Faber & Faber office at 4.00 pm while he finished a meeting about Stockhausen (the substance of which was not revealed to me). Eventually I was called in, and he seemed relieved to be able to take some time out to talk about Mahler. There were plans for another new edition of the Alma Mahler *Memories and Letters*, and he had talked about Henry Louis de La Grange, whose new book (the first volume of which came out a month or so later) he had seen; he was impressed by the biographical 'scoops', but less sure about the musical discussion or the volume's broadly 'academic' standing. My diary notes about the meeting suggest that we talked about my plans for more concentrated work on the Third Symphony. He told me about the Mengelberg Collection in The Hague, which he was shortly going to visit, and the manuscript of the Third in the Pierpont Morgan Library in New York. We parted very cordially after he had taken down my address and telephone number.

It turned out to be quite a year. A month or so after returning from a holiday in Austria and Italy, I was interviewed for a job teaching Music History and beginners' German at a college for American students taking their junior year abroad. I was offered it just a week or two before heading back up to York to receive my D.Phil. at the formal degree ceremony in July. By mid-August I had left the Civil Service and left London for the American college, which was housed in a Victorian country mansion, soon to be purchased by the Midwestern university that ran it. There I was to embark upon what would eventually turn into a *bona fide* academic career. The teaching at first was relatively basic, but fun, and the students bright and entertaining. By the second year I was chancing my arm on an 'English Music' survey course that most definitely included Britten.

Teaching Opera. Britten's Death. Mahler and Donald Mitchell

The secret pleasures of studying and really 'getting to know' large-scale musical works – like symphonies and operas – are available to all but appreciated by few. How to come to terms with an opera had been a necessary discovery for me, as a solitary A-level student faced with Verdi's *Rigoletto* and guided by a youthfully enthusiastic but performance-orientated music teacher who was also making it up as he went along. I discovered the absorbing possibility of 'reading' such a work as one might read an engrossing novel, but in successive stages or 'layers'. Time would be spent experimentally following the route the composer must have taken to produce a finished score that could be made sense of in performance. First might come the source, which, in the case of opera by the mid-nineteenth century, could well have been a popular novel or stage play. From that would be derived a 'libretto', a text, usually produced by a literary or drama specialist of some kind, occasionally by the composer (as with Wagner). Then, thanks not only to the published libretto and vocal score, along with the luxury of endlessly repeatable modern recordings, one might explore the completed opera scene by scene, act by act, listing significantly recurring musical material (themes, figures or self-contained gestures) and mapping its dramatic and emotional trajectory. Key landmarks would be its spaces of repose, its moments of dramatic or 'melodramatic' action. How were these tailored to accommodate significant musical 'moments', arias or set pieces, while allowing characters to communicate musically? Are the formal, meditatively 'slow', listener-orientated monologues of Wagner's Wotan, or the faster, even nearly conversationally paced stretches of dialogue in Richard Strauss conditioned by or extraneous to an underlying musical structure that involves repetition and 'form'?

There is nothing that better encourages the devotion of time to this process than knowing you are going to have to 'teach' such works: to communicate something of the pleasure you have derived from an opera you might be introducing to a class of non-specialist American 'liberal arts' students who have just come from the pottery studio and will later attend a History class on the Tudor monarchy. Of course you must contextualize and explain quite a lot before playing carefully selected 'highlight' moments; in the process you might hope to inspire just one or two to follow the route of discovering such things for themselves.

I found myself not only enjoying teaching as much as I had hoped I would but also utilizing the opportunities provided for getting to know Wagner, Puccini and, indeed, Britten operas for the various courses I began to devise. Sometimes these were linked to actual trips into London to see works we had discussed. In those days one could still secure a decent block of centre stalls seats at Covent Garden on a reduced-price 'educational' group-booking arrangement. ENO productions at the Coliseum were even easier. It was in those years of the mid- to late 1970s that I really 'got to know' the *Ring* cycle and explored operas for the English Music survey course that would include *Billy Budd* and, one memorable year, *Peter Grimes*.

I taught the latter in the first semester (running from mid-August to early December) of the 1976–7 academic year. By then I had gained deeper, more systematically acquired knowledge of the opera that may well have coloured my attempt to recapture earlier the memory of my first experience of it in the theatre in 1967. In its turn, that experience very definitely influenced the last of my two or three classes devoted to it, with a faithful and engaged group of particularly good students. That evening I had offered a listen-through of the complete Decca recording, in an informal, and optional, 'bring-your-own-cushion' session. It was scheduled to begin a little after dinner that evening. Before going down to eat, I had turned on the radio. It was 16th November 1976. I was shocked to hear the newsreader announce that the composer Benjamin Britten was "gravely ill." I wondered if I might, as a result, find *Grimes* too much to take in the light of that unexpected report, for all that it was well known that he had been ill ever since the heart operation three years earlier. I had of course since seen him, frail and with a stick, being supported by Donald Mitchell at the 1973 *Death in Venice* performance that I attended. Might I fall victim to what Chowrimootoo would no doubt call "sickly sentimentality"?

Deciding that whatever emotions it might arouse would probably be appropriate, I went ahead with the session; listening to *Peter Grimes* seemed the best sort of homage we could pay in the circumstances. It was indeed a moving experience. I had begged the students to remember that they had been studying this remarkable opera while its composer lay seriously ill and possibly dying (the newsreader had not said as much, but the implication was clear from the very fact that the state of health of a mere composer should figure in the evening bulletin). Much later, after Grimes had been consigned to the waves and the students had gone, I had turned the radio back on for the late evening news. "Lord Britten" (the title had been bestowed earlier in the year) was "said to be seriously ill, his condition giving his friends cause for great concern. . . . He is 62."

That was Tuesday. By Wednesday his poor state was linked to "a deteriorating heart condition" by those with him at his home in Aldeburgh. By the weekend, term had ended, and I was back for Christmas with my parents in London. The reports did not alter but faded somewhat from the bulletins, although I looked forward to a scheduled TV film about Britten, which included a long interview with Peter Pears. It had been recorded earlier in the year, perhaps to mark his birthday on 22nd November, but now had the feeling of a kind of farewell. However, it was not until Saturday, 4th December that I recorded in my diary:

> 6.15 pm I have just heard the radio news. Britten died today, aged 63, at Aldeburgh.

That evening the tributes began, and in the following days I made sure to gather in some of the papers carrying obituaries and memorial pieces. Later would come Tippett's extraordinarily moving essay that had been broadcast on Radio Three and was subsequently printed in *The Listener* (on 16th December). On the 7th of December both BBC and ITV ran filmed footage of the funeral. It caught Pears, standing tall as ever; I noted in my diary that he had seemed to be telling a middle-aged woman (one of Britten's sisters? – or was it faithful nurse Rita who had accompanied him in the procession to the grave?) when to throw her flowers onto the interred coffin:

> with his massive features ... tightened in some profound complexity of grief as the coffin was lowered into the grave. Vere, not Aschenbach now.

* * *

The following term brought an unexpected moment of posthumous contact with Britten's circle. More tributes and recollections, in various forms and media, had inevitably followed his death. My sporadic diary entries caught a touching radio interview with Pears on Sunday, 27th February 1977 in the rather awkward context of a half-hour programme of various items related to the theme 'God and Music'. The Pears interview was the most memorable:

> there was Pears, describing what 'God' meant to him ... and saying that Ben Britten and his music had been the 'centre' of his life. Did that mean, then (the interviewer thrust it in with only a sight touch of 'due respect' in the tone of his voice) that his life *had* no centre now? No ... the music was still there, Ben was still there in that sense. ... Since his death he had been singing only *his* music ... *St Nicolas* in Cardiff the day after the funeral; but for all the pain it had been worthwhile – the audience and other players 'with' him, and Ben there too. (Something in his voice at this point suggested that emotion had begun to get the better of him). What final piece of music would he choose (the interviewer went on)? " 'God moves in a mysterious way' from *St Nicolas* ... to believe that is to gain some way of holding on. ... I may cry, but ..." And so the interview ended with the hymn fading in behind Pears's words of sorrow. Deeply moving, perhaps *because* of the triteness of the context. ... One must cope somehow – that is his way, carried on by the memory of Ben's claim to a mutual friend that his music became more and more a matter of "praising God". ... I wonder.

After all the tributes and obituaries, Britten and his music slipped again into the background of my life at that time. I was considering my 'career', given the inevitable lack of any real possibility of progression in my current post (which depended upon yearly contracts). This meant writing, trying to get things published. The occasional article about matters relating to Mahler was indeed making it into print at that time, as shortly would another, larger undertaking involving Mahler. The surprise re-connection with Britten actually came with the sudden announcement by our college principal that the artist John Piper would be visiting on one of his many trips to English country houses that figured in an ongoing project devoted to painting them in different seasons. The series already included some memorable, quasi-impressionistic images of our manor from various viewpoints and in differing light conditions. The principal thought that Piper might be intending to make some more sketches of the building. More exciting still was an invitation to the principal's cottage for a dinner on Monday, 18th April, at which John Piper would be present, along with a local cleric who knew him; it was to be a relatively small affair, and I recall only the art historian and me being invited from the resident faculty, although others evidently were. In the wake of that dinner, I made my first diary entry for a month:

> I must clearly record the visit this evening of John and Myfanwy Piper (the latter unexpectedly accompanying the Revd. T. and her husband). Twelve of us had dinner at the principal's. . . . I talked to Piper about Britten from the start, and then was eventually able to get to Mrs Piper for a while on the tour of the house after dinner. At least I was able to offer my admiration of *Death in Venice* and to talk a little about it. Piper himself: not tall, but slender, weathered with white, white hair – a small but handsome figure. Myfanwy: shortish and rather broad . . . and thinning, straight hair – a sort of girls' school headmistress. He observed (amongst other fascinating bits and pieces of information and recollections) that Britten had in the last year of his life come round to *Wagner* somewhat. . . . But no time to record it all now.

Sadly so, since much has now gone, although I do recall talking to him about Britten's recording of *The Dream of Gerontius* and, more generally, the sense of affection and closeness with which Piper spoke of him as a friend and collaborator of many decades. What I most clearly recall of that evening was when our loved but occasionally blundering principal had suddenly produced a wad of what proved to be prints of one of Piper's images of our manor that he had managed to obtain from the publisher of a calendar in which it had figured (I think it had a different Piper image for each month):

> Well, sir, I wonder if I might ask if you would be kind enough to put a signature on these so that we could keep them to give as presents to guest speakers and important visitors to the Manor?

The college's art historian and I could only contain our embarrassed mortification as we watched Piper's face move through surprise and then a flicker of indignation to mildly resigned agreement. "Oh, well, yes, I suppose so . . ." The upside of that embarrassment was that the principal – who would indeed, for some time to come, offer guests a rolled and beribboned copy of "The Piper Print" – had subsequently given me and the art historian each a signed copy. My own now hangs proudly in the hall of my house: a beautiful, glowing image with its two signatures, one printed, the other added in our presence that evening.

* * *

The sad but inexorable momentum of Britten's last year and the effects, both emotional and social, that it chanced to have on my own life have carried me somewhat ahead of other and slightly earlier experiences that merit inclusion here. The first of them would be the second Covent Garden performance of *Death in Venice* that I attended in June 1975. It was in fact the first of the revival, on Friday, 27th June. I had taken one of my American students with me, and my diary records the enthusiasm with which we added our voices to the energetic applause and acclamation that greeted Pears's performance. He had taken his bows "in white suit (somewhat crumpled) and with rosy made-up cheeks and blackened hair and moustache." I was in some respects, however, disappointed by the production on this occasion:

> It was good to see it again – although all in all the performance and staging were if anything less accomplished on this occasion than when I saw it the first time. Added back-projection (the opening scene) did not really add a great deal – the 'Feast of the Sun' walk into the empty stage now had blue- and sand-crayoned bands which are, in my opinion, a mistake. But Pears, while not in his best voice (some thin moments and near breaks in Act I) was as magnificent as ever – his great personality imposing itself even when the actual *acting* is not particularly special – a great *naturalness* is felt throughout, as if indeed . . . he were simply 'playing himself'. The great musical moments became still clearer: the 'view', and the calling of "Adzio!" – "Tadzio!" in Act I; the Prelude to Act II, the incomparable "Socrates knew . . ." (surely the nexus of the whole thing, of Britten vis-à-vis Pears. . . . Will anyone ever be able to do this in the way he does?); and then, of course, the final, heart-breaking droops and aspirations of the strings as Tadzio gestures towards the horizon and dances slowly away into eternity, leaving Aschenbach-Pears slumped dead in his deck-chair at the front (right of the stage). A last, fragile, high harmonic and the vision has gone, it is all over.

All too briefly and imprecisely, these notes indicate that John Piper had been invited to respond to some of the criticism (misguided I feel) of the first production for the relative austerity of its visual aspect. The blue- and sand-crayoned slashes across the previously clear white backcloth for the 'Feast of the Sun' were, as I recall, pretty much re-evoked in the lower part of the front cover of the Faber Vocal Score (the final scene was subsequently re-staged for Tony Palmer's *A Time there Was*[2] – apparently the only section of the 'original' production preserved on film).

Nearly two months later I had taken my parents to a Promenade Concert (we sat in the stalls to the left of the platform, with which we were almost in line). On 21st August Colin Davis had conducted Schubert's Fifth and

Sibelius's First Symphony. But an invaluable extra item, following the Schubert, was the Britten *Serenade*, sung (was it for the last time?) by Pears:

> ageing indeed, yet still a handsome and striking figure of such remarkable presence: a black velvet dinner jacket, a sweeping head of silver hair. Perhaps the power is less, as the ability to get round "excellently bright" . . . but Pears entire and radiant for all that. If the look of staring possession, of mysterious vision and telling now takes on a more frankly old-man's-eye quality, the protestation of fond old age, the agony and depth of humanity also has new and deeper resonances: "our echoes roll from soul to soul" (strong, still able to fill an Albert Hall!), the incomparable Elegy, the high ghostly piping and spooking tone of the Dirge. Finally the radiant Keats sonnet. Will anyone ever sing it so when he is gone?

* * *

I have indicated that Britten was not a central concern of my academic or even recreational musical life at that time in the mid-1970s, except when I was teaching my English Music course. Work on a book on Mahler's Third Symphony was otherwise occupying me. That would only come to fruition much later, but the project played its part in strengthening my re-established contact with Donald Mitchell. In the October of 1975, towards the end of my third semester at the college, I was invited to the launch of Mitchell's second Mahler volume – *Gustav Mahler: The Wunderhorn Years*. This must have happened on Monday, 27th October in Faber's offices at 3 Queen Square. Still rather a shy novice at such events and lacking the 'networking' skills they should have mobilized, I nevertheless found it highly interesting, not least on account of the inevitable presence of members of the Britten circle, and tried to make a decent record of it in my diary. This began with Donald's cordiality in the two brief conversations we had. I pick up the entry from the main speech, made by Robert Donington, who had been introduced in witty 'literary' fashion by one of the Faber directors. What would he say about this notoriously curious volume, whose undoubted fund of interesting information was mostly located in footnotes of gargantuan length glossing relatively short sections of text? (I had made sure to furnish myself with a copy in advance, just to get a flavour of what it held and to ponder what I might say to its author):

> Talking somewhat about Life and Art, Mahler's relevance vis-à-vis the modern 'crisis of confidence', he hit the right sort of note for my taste – but being a totally unexpected kind of person (elderly, very English in a self-effacing, fob-chain-and-flapping-trousers sort of way) and – as he went on . . . and on (to the discomfort of some) – he allowed himself more than one remark that was nothing if not double-edged. He dwelt particularly on Donald's tendency to go 10 miles round after one small butterfly of fact but went on to balance against this DM's skill as a writer. He seemed,

though, never to convince us, or himself, that the 'important' broader view *was* successfully attained in the end. All rather curious, particularly since it came after a 'personal' admission that he (RD) considered *Strauss* to be the one who really succeeded in reconciling the great contrarieties.

Speeches aside (DM making a brief reply and concluding with a toast to the memory of Mahler himself) my partying activities were restricted to talking to DM's brother, to an elderly English musicologist of VW fame (A. E. F. Dickinson) and a somewhat drunken economist I had known at York. Some notables present: Deryck Cooke in brown, Raymond Leppard with friend, and finally (a late arrival) *Peter Pears*.

It is odd to think that Britten was still alive at that point. Much reduced by illness, he had nevertheless just completed *Phaedra* and was already working on the Third String Quartet. My next recorded communication from Donald Mitchell took the form of an extraordinarily encouraging letter, in June 1977, six months after Britten's death (he was, of course, one of the executors of his will). This commended me on the two chapters I had sent him from my book on the Third Symphony. He was enthusiastic about them and wanted us to meet up in July to talk about it and the possibility of publication. We met, in fact, on 12th July at Faber's, where I had to wait for him to arrive, while phone calls came in for him linked to a crisis at Covent Garden, where they had managed to lose a file of Britten obituaries. When he finally appeared, our conversation proved highly significant – not in respect to publishing the Third Symphony book, which seemed still a 'possibility', but consigned to a back burner in favour of a quite new proposition: that I might edit the Dika Newlin translation – which Donald claimed to have had in a drawer for the better part of ten years – of Natalie Bauer-Lechner's *Recollections of Gustav Mahler*. Faber wanted to publish it in 1979.

That summer was a complicatedly significant one. My parents' impending retirement move from outer London down to Sussex had involved the draining task of going through their loft, weeding out things that could be got rid of. But the Bauer-Lechner project, while not the sort of thing I had ever envisaged doing, was a gift for which I remain eternally grateful to Donald. It would give me something more tangible to offer future employers on my otherwise still rather thin list of scholarly publications. For me, then, a new start, even as the life of my other influential provider of musical pleasure had so recently ended.

Notes

1 The singer was Dumitru Brebenel. The conductor was Karl-Frits Voigtmann; director Walter Felsenstein, designer Rudolf Heinrich.
2 Tony Palmer's Prix Italia Prize film about Benjamin Britten, *A time there was* . . . , appeared in 1979 and was reissued in 2006 (Isolde Films).

7 Essay

Travels. Towards Musical Meaning (The *Serenade for Tenor, Horn and Strings*)

I reach a point where the autobiographical strain of this study must reconfront recent 'middlebrow' scholarship and the constructed historical context it has adopted:

> In one camp were the "lowbrows", whose imagined desire for mindless entertainment was supposedly exploited by shamelessly commercial companies, in the other, "highbrows", epitomized by the emerging modernists, were said to shun the offerings of mass culture in favor of aesthetic autonomy, originality, and difficulty. Yet from the beginning the battle lines were complicated by the "middlebrows" – those artists, mediators, and audiences who sought to combine these putatively oppositional aims.[1]

I am unconvinced by this, certainly that it retained any relevance to the musical-cultural world in which I was finding my way in the 1960s and '70s, however glossed by 'imagined', 'supposedly' and 'said to' (by whom?). I would certainly wish to complicate those imagined battle lines as related to the music I valued as an apparent middlebrow, already seeking to explore its qualities with my American students, first in the UK and then, for a fascinating exchange semester that my college facilitated, in a small 'liberal arts' college in the Midwest of America. One work I was particularly keen to discuss with my students in the boldly named town of Liberty, Missouri, was Britten's *Serenade for Tenor, Horn and Strings*, written in 1943 for Pears and the horn player Denis Brain. I am bound to write about it with some degree of sentimentality – but of a kind that is a function of what I will call the 'erotics' of the process of getting to know such a work.

The opening quotation is from Chowrimootoo and Guthrie's Introduction to their JAMS Colloquy devoted to 'Musicology and the Middlebrow', in which Professor Richard Taruskin latterly sought to assure us that Chowrimootoo's 'middlebrowing' of Britten's modernism need *not* in itself be taken as an attack. He then shared with us (highly relevantly to me) something of his own experience as a "lower (receiving) middlebrow" who "ascended to upper (dispensing) middlebrow, the category that takes in professors to the extent that we actually profess." In the process, he felt that he had acquired "social attitudes" that he had "had to unlearn."[2] He had, however, previously reminded us of his Introduction to the *Oxford History*, in which he had suggested "that we ask of music not 'What does it mean?' but 'What has it meant?'."[3] Much as I value that Introduction, I worry now about the move to consign musical meaning to the past, retaining the old masterful ways of conventional musicology in its reliance upon the knowledge of history, of music's past, in a world in which the profession of any currently experienced 'meaning' of specific musical works must be confronted in private and only between consenting adults (what does that remind me of?). Non-performance-based musicology has come to depend upon historical and 'cultural' study, upon the psychology of musical experience (as a 'symptom' of something? – as a problem to be solved, or even immunized against in these pandemic times?). We study performance and performers and leave it, perhaps, to pop-musicologists occasionally to indulge in analyzing their own relationships with albums or videos, with *what* their singer-performers perform, and how, and perhaps why.

'We', the meaningfully disinherited, of course are advisedly fearful of being seen to fall into the trap of 'highbrow' canonic subservience, of being indoctrinated by things we were sold as un-representationally 'pure' – things that now resound anew with the noise of battle, of colonialism and empire, of the racial partisanship and patriarchal dominance that was once hidden under cover of the reverential aesthetic darkness conjured by the notion of 'autonomy'. It is to the almost inevitably implied erotics of those 'in the dark' undercover encounters with works as 'expression', as 'communication', as responses to 'the world' (like so much art of so many cultures) that I am drawn, sustained by disbelief in those neatly segregated historical 'taste' categories proposed by Chowrimootoo and Guthrie. Professor Taruskin appeared resonantly to support their reading of the 'emerging' early twentieth-century modernists as the new highbrows. But I am entirely with him when he mocks "the standard modernist narrative" as "highbrow at its very purest,"[4] except that my memory of the 1960s and early '70s would lead me to insist on adding to these new modernist 'highbrows' the additional, possibly rude, possibly redemptive qualifier: 'pseudo'.

The modernist composers at York in the early '70s, and the European or American innovators they celebrated (like Stockhausen and Boulez, or Cage on more light-hearted days) were in fact nothing if not *anti*-highbrow, in the sense of the other, much commoner understanding of that term as relating 'brow' to social class. Historically the highbrows (as Schumann had already concluded by the 1830s[5]) were the philistine bourgeois types who had most fully internalized the myths of the similarly 'emerging' culture gurus. They were found in posh clothes in the expensive seats in the opera houses that Boulez famously wanted to blow up. The modernists, the avant-garde, were anti-highbrow in the sense that, like Schoenberg, they sought to insert themselves into the Great Tradition as its idealistically truer heirs – albeit as iconoclasts and opera-house terrorists who would be more likely to see themselves as revolutionaries, mocking the old 'highbrows' by shocking, or more accurately, abandoning them and their values as decadent, irrelevant, played out. . . . Chowrimootoo's undercover conflation of 'modernist' with 'highbrow' serves to obscure the fact that the problem his selected critics have with Britten is not that his music amalgamates and confuses high- and lowbrow musical manners so much as that it implicitly mocks the modernists' new-style 'autonomy' and 'purity' (problematic as ever those categories must be). By adopting their anti-highbrow constructional strategies (like dodecaphonic processes) to generate obviously old-style aesthetic effects – to enlarge the expressive vocabulary of his fundamentally vernacular tonal language – Britten threatened to reveal the 'Gothic horror' elements that were always already present in Schoenberg or *The Rite of Spring*. That's why the hardcore modernists hated Britten: for revealing how they did what they did, even while sharing some of their revolutionary ideals and, indeed, articulating them in ways that the 'lower' middlebrows (as Taruskin calls them) found insufferably *highbrow* – like his accent, like the public-schoolboy types he consorted with and the 'bohemian' things they got up to (or were thought to get up to).

It was all just so much more complicated; as was the reception of his music by its *supposedly* 'middlebrow' audience, who took the dissonance and, well, 'modernism' on the chin for the sake of what Chowrimootoo would call the "sickly sentimentality" of the vernacular expressive context that relied upon tonality – the language people 'understood', as Britten put it in his Aspen Award speech.[6] He failed only to admit to saying some rather original and powerful things *in* it that they might be likely to comprehend even while refusing straightforwardly to endorse them. That was the genuinely 'modern' challenge with which his music often presented its audience. But on the matter of audience, I must register something else from the same paragraph as my initial quotation from Chowrimootoo and Guthrie. 'Middlebrow' classical music, its popularizers, promoters and record companies, they insist, targeted audiences

> who looked to culture for aesthetic education, social elevation, and spiritual edification.[7]

Here the prize goes to those who spot what is missing from this list, characterizing the motivation of victims of middlebrow 'improvement'. Education, social elevation and spiritual edification fit nicely the neo-colonialist image of the gullible mass mindlessly sucking up what will really give them no more than a *feeling* of being 'improved', 'educated', 'uplifted', etc. (while no doubt whispering to each other the famous question: "What should I be *listening for*?"). The missing item of the benighted audience's responses to 'culture' in musical form is, quite simply (or rather complicatedly?), *pleasure*, standing perhaps for 'entertainment', in an entirely non-trivial understanding of that term. This is where my insistence on the 'erotics' of becoming familiar, *intimate* with musical works that attract, interest and move us becomes relevant. I think Chowrimootoo gets it – but is this why he has to decry such communicative pleasure as both 'sentimental' and, inevitably, 'sickly'?

I was still inhabiting a period response to all this largely still-unformalized (although practised) criticism from the pseudo-highbrow modernists when, in December 1978, on the verge of heading off to Missouri with my anxiously compressed course notes, I had started to listen to a tape I had made of Britten's *Paul Bunyan* (1941), which opens with the wonderful chorus of 'Old Trees'. Auden's simple lines are supported by what is really just a series of parallel triads. *The Sound of Music* (1959) was not so far away over the hills:

> Since the birth
> Of the earth
> Time has gone
> On and on

This inspired an enthusiastic diary entry, which must now, I suppose, be read as energetic middlebrow partisanship:

> Great fun, particularly the first act, where all is very fresh. And oh that first chorus!! There it is, pure and unadulterated. Dear Ben . . . and Schoenberg still alive in LA! What a wonderful thing it is.

Of course, it *wasn't The Sound of Music*, and did not achieve the popular success Britten and Auden had hoped for – just as the 'pseudo-highbrow' modernists were more modernist than highbrow. Indeed, I must reiterate that 'brow' boasting played little part in discussion of taste in those times. The very notion was largely ignored as a vestige of pre-modernist cultural baggage. At York in 1971–2, Mahler was admired by the undergraduates I was occasionally beginning to teach neither as high- nor lowbrow, but for the extent to which (and I well recall the phrase) he "took the piss out of himself."

Well, they were on to *something* there – but hardly relevant to Britten in a work like the *Serenade*, to which I must return in order to better articulate *in what* my own sense of pleasure in that work consisted. It was primarily derived from a sense of being addressed by an intentional communicator in a medium which, like others deemed conventionally to merit being regarded as 'languages', utilizes a kind of shared vocabulary. It is an oft-repeated linguistic truism that, whether in English, German, Arabic or whatever, there is no inevitable or self-evident link between symbols, sounds and meanings beyond what is granted by those who share them in a cultural community, who have *created it* over time. They will eventually change and extend it on the basis of a broadly shared sense of underlying syntactical, grammatical, 'conventional' means of understanding the ways its elements are linked into phrases, sentences, paragraphs, etc. The connection between 'dog', 'chien' or 'Hund' and a four-legged animal we broadly recognize requires, for example, no primarily 'psychological' explanation. 'Meaning' in this sense is always provisional, local, cultural. Musical meaning is no different; it too can be learned or acquired, its always imprecise translation (where necessary) argued over, refined in a multiplicity of versions – their variety inflected by shared genealogy. Rarely do they register a dog where a cautious cat prowls.

A song cycle is a pre-contextualized example of where and how we might locate the meaningfulness of music – and for this very reason that archautonomist Hanslick confessed that a purist such as he could strictly not accept set text as 'music' at all.[8] I would argue that the songs that make up Britten's *Serenade for Tenor, Horn and Strings* bear a greater burden of meaning than resides 'simply' in the words they set; those words themselves require interpretative work from the seeker after meaning and meaningful pleasure. Poetry requires familiarity with idioms, with how language was used in the period in which it was written, with metaphor, with forms and conventions of rhetoric in which the 'musicking' of language merges into the meaningfulness of music.

In the first song of the cycle,[9] the setting of Cotton's 'Pastoral', we accept the figurative, but literally nonsensical, idea that a day can age, that the sun can 'faint', with or without 'steeds' or 'chariot'. Cultural as well as linguistic knowledge is required for understanding poetry as much as music. In a similar way, the 'purely musical' horn Prologue demands culturally based imaginative work from us in order to 'hear' the way its conventional call in bar 1 (evoking the functional horns of former hunters, etc.) is incrementally extended into a melodic unit in bars 2 and 3. It relies upon iterations of short figures linked by the initial 'Scotch snap'; the emphasis may fall on the longer held notes, but the solo's weight and significance is marked by the character and pitch of their placement, most prominently on the upper G, the implied dominant. The effect is of a conventional horn 'call' that develops into a kind of wordless recitative that is possessed of increasing urgency. Something of this affects the first 'sentence', that appears to end with the same falling E to C that had concluded the first three-bar phrase. The second sentence is where the B is flattened and the 'animando' crescendo introduces an urgent climb to the first prominent F, which will sound 'out of tune' as a result of the player using the natural harmonics that Britten asks for in a footnote to the score. A pause emphasizes the 'call'-like character of the rise from C to G, repeated with an upper appoggiatura (A to G). The final two bars slow to a close on the same E to C termination, its finality now stressed by falling to the *lower* C, a full octave and a third, as it dies away.

The symbolic 'call' of the horn has become ever more pressingly articulate, but the natural harmonics add a curiously alien quality to its eloquence, as if the instrument's association with human encroachment upon nature has become one *with* a nature that is somehow beyond 'us' as we now are, or think we are. The first song, the Cotton 'Pastoral', finds the urgency of the Scotch snap figure calmed into a gentle repeat-pattern accompaniment – soothing as a lullaby – to the tenor's evocation of the effects of the approaching sunset, with its contrasting, pizzicato-accompanied 'middle section' for the little flock of sheep, before the strings more conventionally accompany the tenor's final lines describing the conversing locals, awaiting the sunset and their beds.

The second song, the Tennyson 'Nocturne', brilliantly evokes fairy-tale castle walls lit splendidly by the late sun – the Scotch snap is now once more a kind of call: it introduces the thematization of *sound* in, if not precisely *of*, nature, the eagerly blown bugle (mimicked in lively fashion by the solo horn) setting the wild echoes flying and dying. The singer, as poet, then addresses us, directing us to hear and *listen to* the famous echoes of the "horns of elfland faintly blowing." The physical echoes may die, but for all that (as the hopeful poet-listener becomes a communicator, even a lover) "*our* echoes roll from soul to soul," hopefully figured as growing "for ever" even as they dwindle away into a nothingness over which the Scotch snap presides in three quiet, quizzical iterations by three solo violins.

The Blake 'Elegy' I had known since school days, when Harry had introduced us to its luxuriantly bitter knowledge of "the worm in the rose," revealed here upon a comfortable bed of quietly pulsing string chords. The horn plays a foregrounded role, almost *performing* the despoilment of the rose while elaborating upon its own preludial recitative (was *this* the knowledge that had provoked its urgency?). Now it is directly voiced, after the instrumental introduction, by the tenor ("Oh Rose, thou art sick . . .") in an opening passage marked 'Recitativo' – the voice now, perhaps, the voice *of* the horn, of nature itself. Its first two notes perform the major-to-minor third (E major to E minor) with which the real horn will conclude this shockingly beautiful, fatally erotic song – almost literally 'echoing' the musical voice of another composer for whom Britten, too, cared: the Mahler of the Nietzsche setting ("O Man, take heed . . .") in the Third Symphony, where, in its enormous first movement, a solo trombone had similarly played the role of inarticulately eloquent voice, interestingly (for Chowrimootoo?) marked "Sentimental" – but surely evoking Schiller's understanding of that word as 'yearning for' the nature of which the 'naïve' spirit was already a part.[10]

Mahler's take on the German-Romantic dream world of shadowy and sometimes nightmarish visions seems directly referenced in the 'Dirge', where the musical echoes of calling voices are mixed with those of the spirits and spooks of a reanimated mediaeval picturing of what lurks in wait for the uneasy Christian soul, for whom the dark night and its dreams of dread may reveal what death itself could promise. The accompaniment's grotesque fugue is as figuratively 'impure' as 'pure music' can ever be as it all but overwhelms the singer before it shuffles, leaps and claws its way out of sight, past the variously browed souls of Britten's critics now caught in its web. And still the tenor holds to his reiterated "This aye night," concluding with a chilling, undeluded benediction, "And Christ receive thy saule . . ."

In bright contrast, Ben Johnson's 'Hymn' provides a joyful, virtuosic interlude in which the tenor skips and dances before the moon as a shining goddess. Diana the huntress reminds him of the brightness of the day now gone as she aims her shining arrow at the hart, blissfully unaware (as it leaps) of its impending demise. This music renounces individualized subjective 'expression' but projects the differently meaningful animation of dancing bodies – the horn player melodically leaping like the threatened hart, the singer conjuring an image of the pursuing goddess.

The concluding 'Sonnet' by Keats ('To Sleep') loses the role-playing horn altogether and turns back into music as expression, as an explicit form of address. Its primary addressee is not, however, the listener, who now eavesdrops upon a conversation between the singer-poet and music itself as personified sleep inducer ('soothing the savage brow' of whatever height). The poetic conceit is a venerable one, but the character of the string accompaniment is entirely Britten's. As if standing in for the absent horn, the strings seem to have become the metaphorically embodied Sleep, addressed by Keats in a manner that owes much to the Elizabethans. But from the outset, the magical sequence of five major triads, performed by *divisi* violas descending from ethereal realms in two gentle stages (D, C sharp, E flat, C and back to D) above a rising cello bassline, is meaningfully soothing, calming, stilling. It surely "passes a maternal hand over the hair of those to whom it turns" in the way that Adorno would characterize the music of Mahler's Fourth Symphony.[11] Britten's music does all the things Keats asks Sleep to do, or attributes to it the ability to do. But in its performance it is also 'accompaniment', of course: cognizant of images and figures conjured by the poet and 'heard' by a music that enacts its sympathy by imagining metaphorical, 'musical' versions of passing, troubled simulacra like that of the semitonally burrowing mole of 'curious conscience'. Before that it had gathered its resources into a rhetorical gesture of attention-grabbing urgency, a sharply reiterated G major chord with added major seventh: the F sharp that is left hanging beneath the tenor's 'breeding many woes'. A similar gesture halts the accompaniment three bars later at "that still lords its strength for darkness," and then again before the tenor's climactic bidding (has Sleep revealed its family connection with Death?): "Turn the key deftly in the oilèd wards, / And seal the hushèd Casket of my Soul." At this closing line the strings resume their performance, throwing about the poet their "lulling charities" with the quietest reiteration of the three opening chords (D major, C sharp major, E flat major) in a kind of slow ostinato before coming to rest (is it sleep or death?) in the gentlest and most benign D major. At which miraculous moment we realize that the horn has been absent from the stage. In a wonderfully Mahlerian solution, we hear, as Epilogue, the mysteriously repeated solo Prologue, now *off-stage*. The horn has returned to the forest, to nature; the human music, with its protean richness of meaning, has ceased.

Leeds. 'The Open Secret'. Philip Brett and 'A Midsummer Night's Dream'

My UK academic career began in earnest in January 1980, in a new decade and a new location not so far from my old university in York. I had successfully applied for a lectureship in Music at the University of Leeds. The two cities, and universities, were in truth very different. Leeds was a decidedly bigger financial and industrial centre, with a grand Victorian Town Hall; its university was much longer established, with connections to local industry and the world of business. It saw itself as more down-to-earth and egalitarian than York, with its modern design and increasingly 'fashionable', rather arty middle-class atmosphere.

Further experiences of Britten's music were for a time inevitably rendered more sporadic and accidental by my ever-increasing involvement with early twentieth-century Austrian and German music. But the Britten who was irrevocably a part of me – both as a kind of role model and as the creator of so many works that I loved – was still hard to avoid in that busy period of posthumous tributes. There was the wonderful Tony Palmer film *A Time There Was*: in some sense the first significant 'biography' of the composer, first shown in 1980, over ten years before Humphrey Carpenter's influential study of 1992.[12]

Of course the 'open secret' had, in a sense, ceased to be secret with *Death in Venice*. Pioneering 'gay musicologist' Philip Brett had famously tackled the matter with respect to *Peter Grimes* in his groundbreaking article on the opera in *The Musical Times* in December 1977. Nineteen eighty also saw the publication, in the *Observer Review* of Sunday, 3rd March, of Gillian Widdicombe's long article, based on an interview with Peter Pears – instigator of the Tony Palmer film – in which she addressed the matter of their relationship and quoted a subsequently famous observation by Pears, made in the film but published by her in advance of its first broadcast on Easter Sunday by London Weekend Television:

> 'It was established very early that we were passionately devoted and close,' Pears says in the film. 'The word "gay" was not in his vocabulary. . . . Ben thought that decent behaviour, decent manners were part of a fine life. Gracious living, if you like. But "the gay life," he resented that . . . he was more interested in the beauty, and therefore the danger, that existed in any relationship between human beings – man and woman, man and man; the sex didn't really matter.'[13]

There certainly remained much to contend seriously with in what Eve Kosofsky Sedgwick famously called the 'epistemology of the closet' in her 1990 study of that name.[14] Donald Mitchell, with whom I continued to maintain cordial and friendly relations, was long protective of talk about Britten's sexuality and had characteristically launched into his discussion of 'Let the florid music', in his 1981 book *Britten and Auden in the Thirties*, by describing it as one of the very few examples of a serious neo-classicizing spirit in Britten, but the style admirably projects the ceremonial proclamation of the first verse, the public statement.[15]

Of course it is the more obviously 'private' statement of Auden's second verse that demands thought and calls for interpretation in relation to the first ("O but the unloved have had power."). Who are the 'unloved'? – are they other, less articulate admirers of the addressee of the first verse ("Let the florid music praise . . . / Beauty's conquest of your face")? And what is the "striking" that accompanies their weeping? Who are their "secretive children" walking through "your vigilance of breath" (a complex-enough concept in its own right) to "unpardonable death"? And then, at the last, the poet clarifies the gender (of the previously admired beauty?) of the owner of an overpowering "look":

> And my vows break
> Before his look.[16]

As Britten presents the complex text in a cloak of florid musical rhetoric, so Mitchell aided him in his task of defusing the questions in a kind of descriptive 'performance'. The second verse, he observes, "was immeasurably the more difficult task, not only to project private rather than public images but to make a unity of those public and private worlds":

> [Britten] secures his musical unity by unfolding in the second verse the simplest and most transfiguring of modifications of the musical materials (x in the examples). . . . The song's brilliance resides in that compositional process.[17]

As always, 'analysis' comes to the musicologist's aid, not only in avoiding 'meaning' but often actively to deny it – although Mitchell does not explicitly *do* that, and his analysis is interesting enough on its own terms. But he was not above more direct action on Britten's behalf, again often as not with intentions that were fundamentally noble. In the January of my first full academic year at Leeds (in 1981), I had gone down to London to meet him at Faber, and he had taken me out to a very pleasant lunch over which he talked somewhat about his next Mahler book (this would be the 1985 *Gustav Mahler: Songs and Symphonies of Life and Death*) before the conversation moved more directly on to Britten via thoughts about 'oriental' heterophony in *Das Lied von der Erde* and Britten's interest in the gamelan. It then moved onto one of the 'protective' actions to which I have referred. I described the meeting in my diary:

> he had some interesting things to say about *Das Lied* and a 1906 (?) article by Adler on oriental music, with music examples that look not unlike Mahler's material (gamelan music and heterophony). Learning that I was

teaching *Das Lied* myself, Donald readily offered to come up and contribute. So kind he is – although the position from my point of view would have to be carefully weighed. We then went on to Britten somewhat, and he revealed some interesting things: Ronald Duncan's book was *produced*, but then *pulped by the publisher*! (Did Donald have something to do with this [as he had claimed]? He said that some copies did, in fact, get onto the market and were bought, but was keen to explain that Duncan was more or less dotty and a bitter man. The book abounded in errors and so on, though he had a copy which I could see if I wished.)

In the end, I found my own copy in York in 1982 (it is also referenced by Humphrey Carpenter and others), and must confess that Duncan's *Working with Britten: A Personal Memoir* is far from being a wronged masterpiece. It begins, indeed, as a very loosely written series of disjointed observations and recollections, somewhat randomly divided into 'chapters'. Concerning his collaboration with Britten on *The Rape of Lucretia*, he nevertheless has something more to offer. I cannot entirely suppress the suspicion that Donald would particularly have disliked the second chapter's conclusion with a rather unfeeling account of Britten revealing his sexuality to Duncan at the *Mainly Musicians* club in London: "He remained a reluctant homosexual, a man in flight from himself, who often punished others for the sin he felt he'd committed himself. He was a man on the rack."[18]

* * *

I have referred already (see Ch.5, p. 59) to Philip Brett's well-known essay 'Britten's Dream', in which he offers the following analysis of the problem that Britten's beloved boys posed both to him and to us:

> It is of course misleading simply to throw the late nineteenth-century word homosexual, with its implications of pathology and 'medicalization', into the ring with an older and more universal phenomenon of Western paternalistic society that has typically involved the teaching of younger men by older ones, sometimes with an erotic element (as in the case of that prototypical teacher, Socrates) and sometimes not. For modern society, however, pederasty is a dangerous area – the side of paternalism that manifests itself physically becomes 'sexual abuse'.[19]

He went on to observe that Britten himself never suffered the persecution inspiring the "paranoid fears common to most homosexuals" with which he "came to terms in the terrifying manhunts of *Peter Grimes*."[20] He then explored the thematized possibility of a dominant, and sexualized, man-boy relationship in *The Turn of the Screw*. Accepting that Britten seems "never to have forced himself upon his young friends," Brett proposed that the opera's ambiguity does not depend upon whether or not the ghosts exist but springs from a musical question as to how different in kind are the relationships, and which is worse for the poor boy: that with the predatory ghost or with the smothering governess.[21]

The pervasive power and undoubted allure of the dark-side position is most articulately presented in Peter Quint's Act I nocturnal 'conversation' with Miles, the latter wandering 'in his nightgown' in the grounds of Bly while Quint 'addresses' him from its tower:

> I am all things strange and bold,
> The riderless horse
> Snorting and stamping on the hard sea sand,
> The hero-highwayman plundering the land.
> I am King Midas with gold in his hand.
> I am the smooth world's double face,
> Mercury's heels
> Feathered with mischief and a God's deceit.
> The brittle blandishment of counterfeit.
> In me secrets and half-formed desires meet.

Quint's Manichean challenge to divine 'deceit' reveals him to be no mere picture-book dragon or Gothic horror spook. But if the questions continue to hover with the ghosts in *The Turn of the Screw*, other Britten operas permit a more convincingly redemptive alternative than the nervous Governess, wronged, and perhaps herself wronging. We might return to *Billy Budd* in search of a differently articulated balance between the forces of darkness and light, in which both are mediated by a kind of internalized repression.

Claggart is darkly obsessed by Billy's 'handsomeness' *and* 'goodness', feeling psychotically that he must destroy the latter in order to possess or simply cancel the pain of the former in some way – that will of course destroy Billy. To Britten's Vere, not Melville's,[22] it is given to negotiate those of Claggart's and perhaps his own feelings for Billy which cannot be supported by the moral order he represents on *The Indomitable*. They may nevertheless become pointers to the far-sighted sail of salvation that embraces love and forgiveness of the kind that Billy had precisely bestowed upon Vere in his final 'blessing', before being hanged at his command. The crucial lines for Vere are those of his internal monologue after the officers have departed, having given their verdict at the end of the 'drum-head court' in response to Billy's instinctively hurled fist. That was his only spontaneous means of articulating his rejection of Claggart's false accusation of treachery, bribery and mutiny; his stammer prevented any more cautious verbal rebuttal. Vere knows he must accept his officers' verdict, and the death sentence, but feels that he has seen divine goodness at work in that blow that unintentionally felled and killed Claggart. The latter's evil conclusions, with respect to his own feelings about

Billy, now tragically align with what Vere must himself sanction. Procedural propriety becomes one with a kind of moral defeat, the metaphorical 'sinking' of the 'floating monarchy' over which he rules:

> Before what tribunal do I stand if I destroy goodness? The angel of God has struck and the angel must hang – through me. Beauty, handsomeness, goodness, it is for me to destroy you. I, Edward Fairfax Vere, Captain of *The Indomitable*, lost with all hands on the infinite sea.

With this he turns to enter the stateroom into which Billy had been removed while the officers of the court had discussed their verdict. Vere has become a reluctant messenger of death: "How can he pardon? How receive me?" The curtain falls upon the encounter that follows, which we do not see; but it gives rise to what Brett understandably calls "the strangest and most daring moment in the score . . . What we hear are thirty-four clear, triadic chords, each of them harmonizing a note of the F major triad, and each scored differently."[23] It is overwhelmingly one of the great moments of twentieth-century opera. Page 296 of the Boosey and Hawkes vocal score looks almost like a piece by Morton Feldman, yet it is also one of the most powerfully articulate *sentiment* articulating orchestral interludes in opera. The chords are not just differently scored: their relationship with each other is often grammatically startling (F major, A major, D-flat major) and each bears a different dynamic marking: *f, ff, mf, p, mf, fff* and so on.[24] Perhaps only for an audience of intelligent cinema-goers might these chords reveal, as in a sudden series of 'stills' – frozen glimpses of what transpires – the emotions of both Vere and Billy captured in a process that might, as the chords grow quieter and gentler, have involved some level of sympathetic understanding of each other's bitter knowledge, perhaps even of physical contact between them, with Vere attempting to say what ultimately cannot be said other than with an arm tenderly placed around the shoulders of the stricken boy. Perhaps that, as much as Billy's last public 'blessing' of "starry Vere," is what the Captain recalls in his culminatory moment of transfiguration in the Epilogue. There the elderly Vere, still reminiscing, completes his story of what had happened. Anything but some such powerful expression of what might, in the best sense, be called 'sentimentality' would have been inappropriate to the enormity of the recalled drama and how he was able to conceive of 'living with it' in the terms of the society, and the moral order whose representative he believed himself to have been:

> I was lost on the infinite sea, but I've spotted a sail in the storm, the far-shining sail and I'm content. I've seen where she's bound for There's a land where she'll anchor for ever.

* * *

And yet, as we know, there *are* other ways of looking at all this – ways more pitilessly critical of Vere's role and behaviour, like Harper-Scott's (I will return to him), or more accepting of the fact that the Claggarts of this world can, and perhaps do, more often win. Here I must head back to the rather unlikely enchanted woodland of Britten's version of *A Midsummer Night's Dream*, whose libretto he and Pears together derived from the Shakespeare play. It is not the best loved of Britten's works, perhaps because of the prominent boy-fairies – elphin versions, perhaps, of those "thin-as-a-board juveniles"[25] Auden had once mocked Britten for being attracted to. How easily they might embody a kind of false consciousness when we turn to the fear of 'abuse' that is hinted in various judiciously critical aspects of Brett's own consideration of Britten's journey of self-psychological examination. This, he persuasively implies, gave the lie to Montagu Slater's exasperated complaint that the Britten of the first three operas – social dramas about oppression and the way in which the oppressed might internalize "society's condemnation"[26] – was to turn into a kind of "court musician."[27]

For Brett, the composer's subsequent operatic journey from *Billy Budd* (1951) through *Gloriana* (1953) to *The Turn of the Screw* (1954) was worth contextualizing in relation to some very public dramas of the early '50s: like that around the homosexually 'scandalous' aspects of the Burgess and Maclean affair (1951) or the trial (1952) and subsequent suicide of Alan Turing in 1954. Brett accordingly, and perhaps tendentiously, finds the 'danger of being gay' stalking in and out of the shadows of all the works of that period. He even takes a critical line from Eve Kosofsky Sedgwick's extended consideration of Melville's *Billy Budd* (which occasionally cites Britten's) to question whether Vere's Epilogue can be taken at face value. Does the "throbbing pulse of the militaristic music of the earlier sea-chase" that underpins his opening lines highlight the "almost embarrassing epiphanic arrival of an otherwise unclouded B-flat chord"?[28] Does that anticipate Sedgwick's vision of Vere? he asks, citing and locating the passage in which she pictures the captain:

> "retiring from his agonistic public performance, only, alone at last, to hug himself in delight under the covers, getting off on the immutable visual glory of the boy who 'ascending, took the full rose of the dawn'": the excitement of those drumbeats after all, the music obliquely suggests, is not entirely removed from the thrill of orgasm.
>
> (Sedgwick 118)[29]

I must confess to being no more persuaded by this reading than by Chowrimootoo's of the close of Act I of *Death in Venice*. Much might be said about the musically orgasmic, but in neither of these instances would it seem convincingly relevant. Surely the naval-militaristic 'drumbeats' accompanying the beginning of Vere's Epilogue are *funereal* rather than sexual, echoing from the grim assembly of the crew to witness the execution in horror, before the fade back into the drifting sea music of Vere's Prologue. Far more important might be his intuitive near-repetition of *Billy's* visionary lines (unheard by Vere): "I've sighted a sail in the storm, / The far-shining sail that is not fate,"[30] and then the allusion to his private scene with Billy, explaining the verdict, with its great chords. I am, however, much more convinced by Brett's interpretation of *A Midsummer Night's Dream* in the spirit of 1950s Shakespeare scholarship that was, he suggests, repositioning the comedies as 'saturnalian' rather than romantic – the *Dream*'s wood a place in which "to gain release from everyday restraint under the influence of Oberon."[31]

He persuasively describes Oberon, with his uncanny falsetto and king-of-the-fairies costume, as "emasculated, misogynistic, boy-desiring" and "almost literally a figure of the closet"[32] who stands for the archaic world of opera as reappropriated by gay culture. This suggests a curious and possibly disturbing linkage of the pairing of Oberon and Puck – his "henchman," the boy-tumbler who "snaps to his master's attention with even greater alacrity"[33] – with that of the less free-spirited Miles and Quint. Brett omits only to emphasize that link with reference to Quint's most explicit revelation of his sexual designs upon Miles in *The Turn of the Screw*'s ghostly Act Two 'Colloquy' between Quint and Miss Jessel:

> I seek a friend –
> Obedient to follow where I lead,
> Slick as a juggler' mate to catch my thought,
> Proud, curious, agile, he shall feed
> My mounting power.
> Then to his bright subservience I'll expound
> The desperate passions of a haunted heart,
> And in that hour
> "The ceremony of innocence is drowned."

That link surely makes the stigma of abuse one of the shadows of the shadow-filled wood of *A Midsummer Night's Dream*, a performance of which chanced to be the last meeting I had with Harry, the much-loved teacher with whom I had studied the *War Requiem* long ago.

Although brilliant in the classroom and as a choral conductor, he had been drawn into the notionally 'higher' realm of educational administration. His personal life had not been easy, but after retirement he had returned to his love of drama and Shakespeare (he was himself a talented actor, as all good schoolteachers are to some extent) and had become the admired visiting director of a series of Shakespeare plays put on by a former acquaintance (in English) in the language department of a Polish university.

One of his own personal sadnesses had been to know another fine teacher of his generation who had met his gruesome end as the victim of two 'rent boys' who had tortured and murdered him – completing a darkly tragic circle in which a notional abuser became an actual victim of those who, in other circumstances, might have been the abused. Harry had tried to steer him onto another path but ultimately accepted defeat – a defeat that fuelled his own passion to give something back to the young in his Shakespeare productions.

He always remembered my birthday (and those of many others of his former pupils), and a ticket to a March 2018 performance of Britten's *A Midsummer Night's Dream* by ENO at the Coliseum – it was the Robert Carsen production revived from 1995 – was my belated birthday present from him for the previous year. He was generously proud of my move to Oxford in 1996 and knew that I had offered some courses devoted to Britten before retiring in 2014. He wanted, I think, to have another 'Britten experience' in my company. It had been an enjoyable evening, for all that he was evidently slowing down, feeling his age and suffering from knee trouble that necessitated the use of a stick. We both found things to admire in the performance, which was lively and sensitive in its way, for all that it was overshadowed in my mind by another ENO production of the same opera, to which I will shortly turn. That March 2018 evening shared with Harry was to be the last time I saw him. A sudden and unexpected heart attack snatched him away that August. To the great sadness of that was added the more minor yet significant one about which I had spoken to him over our meal in the subterranean restaurant in the Coliseum: I would have loved to re-experience with him the 2011 production that I knew would have touched and fascinated him. In this respect I am all the more sorry that it was not the one revived, but can guess the reasons.

We know from Shakespeare, of course, that the fairy kingdom of the forest, into which the human lovers bring their desires and confusions, is troubled by a dispute between Oberon and his queen Titania over a "lovely boy" – a changeling, whom Oberon wants Titania to relinquish to him. Given the misgivings of some about Britten's opera, it may be understood why, having torn myself away from a busy end-of-year examination period in June 2011 for an evening's escape into operatic magic, I had been disquieted by the programme book for Christopher Alden's production (whose initial reviews I had not followed). Its shiny cover was filled with a greenish-blue tinted, rather artfully processed photograph of a crowd of small boys in shorts, laughing and jostling or restraining each other as they appeared to be about to storm forwards towards the camera, in the otherwise cheerless playground of a cheerless-looking school.

In the centre foreground, at some distance from the boys behind him, stands an unsmiling, apparently insouciant fair-haired boy whose arms are tightly crossed about his chest, perhaps self-protectively (his hands invisible beneath the arms of his school jumper). His neat school tie has slightly slipped below the unbuttoned collar of his well-ironed shirt; he is visible from the waist up. Is his blank expression that of someone defensively expecting to be blamed for something, or does it challenge us on behalf of the unruly crowd

Essay 93

Figure 7.1 A black-and-white reproduction of the ENO Programme cover for Christopher Alden's 2011 production of *A Midsummer Night's Dream*.

Source: (ENO design team, Copyright of the English National Opera – by permission)

behind him? Thumbing quickly on through the programme for some sort of enlightenment in the ten minutes or so before the performance was to begin, I was further disquieted to see that the synopsis was followed by an essay by John Bridcut called 'A Precocious Schoolboy', although it looked (and was) typically sensitive and interesting in addressing Britten's own memories of himself as a schoolboy and dealing with his treatment of Puck as "a raw street urchin who behaves with the vital spontaneity that so appealed to Britten in boys."[34] He went on to suggest that it was hard to conceive of Puck as entirely "innocent," but subsequently recorded the testament of Stephen Terry, who had known, and 'known about' Britten at school but "detected nothing sexual in Britten's behaviour towards him, only 'an incredible tenderness'."[35] It is relevant here also to recall the judicious way in which John Bridcut dealt, in *Britten's Children*, with Eric Crozier's later, embittered recollections of the composer which included the claim that Britten had himself confided in Crozier about being sexually abused as a schoolboy. However unsubstantiated, that widely circulated suggestion troublingly coloured the piece that followed Bridcut's in the programme.[36] Titled 'A Suitable Boy', it was extracted from an *Observer Magazine* essay, and glossed in somewhat tabloid fashion:

> In 2001, after a silence of more than 30 years, Don Boyd confronted the painful memories of being sexually abused at school.[37]

Anxiety about what we were in for was in no way dispelled when the curtain rose upon a bleak schoolyard like that in the programme book's cover photograph. It was bordered on two sides by a grim-looking school building, two storeys high and obscuring any view of the outside world or landscape; not a tree or even a flowerpot in sight. It was evidently going to be one of 'those' productions – imposing a 'reading' upon an opera and its audience, often bizarrely and deliberately jarring with aspects of the action and references in the libretto, and rigorously banning any stage 'magic' of the kind that we are supposed critically to have outgrown (no doubt as 'middlebrow' self-indulgence or 'sentimentality'). But the performance was high-quality, and my sentimental anger at this new imposition of modernist 'austerity' on a once-loved work softened somewhat as it proceeded towards what was rightly hailed as a considerable *coup de théâtre* towards the end of Act II (where the single interval was placed). Here the chaos of the deliberately confused lovers was accompanied by the truly anarchic chaos of a school rebellion that set the school building alight with disturbingly real (and real-smelling) flames in all of the windows, where people could be seen running to and fro to evacuate the boys.

I may not have been the only person in the audience to tense myself for a possible need to exit the theatre if this got out of hand. But the flames were dowsed and the boys led out to congregate in a long (was it double?) line across the stage. Then it was that the magic happened, in the moment that

I have always waited eagerly for since that first production I had seen in East Berlin. Philip Brett writes ambivalently about the appropriation by the boy fairies, in the Britten and Pears libretto, of Puck's lines (in Shakespeare), which he quotes before commenting on Britten's setting of them:

> Jack shall have Jill,
> Nought shall go ill
> The man shall have his mare again
> And all shall be well

Britten gives this speech to the boy fairies, who sing it to a shapely melody in thirds over rapturous repetitions in the orchestra of the four 'motto chords' of the act. The irony of Shakespeare is thus replaced by a statement of faith, if not quite of resolution.

In Auden's terms, of course, this trait was a symptom of the composer's "denial of the demands of disorder." Certainly when the evening's magic has worn off the critical listener will wonder about this passage.[38]

But not, perhaps, on this occasion. Brett had moved from this observation into Chowrimootoo territory, citing the (dangerous?) attraction of Britten's "knife-edge" balance "between the genuine and the sentimental, between honesty about life's difficulties and a longing for resolution and comfort."[39] I would question how problematically specific to Britten that knife edge is – and once again: what precisely might be the difference between the 'genuine' and the 'sentimental'? Might the conclusion of Act II possess a power and genuineness of sentiment to challenge Brett's question? John Bridcut, in his programme-book essay, had compared the "troubling spell" of the opening ten minutes of *A Midsummer Night's Dream* with the "taut soprano glitter of *The Turn of the Screw*," adding:

> in Britten's mind Shakespeare's fairies, far from being 'innocent nothings', had 'a kind of sharpness': the spirit world, he said, was evil as well as good. He also knew that small boys, far from being the angelic, surpliced innocents of fond adult imagination, often possess a cruel *Lord of the Flies* streak.[40]

There was indeed in Alden's bare, treeless schoolyard production a most movingly scary *and* sentimental, good-and-evil sharpness about that wayward, fragile benediction from the lined-up boys who had just burned their school down, tears glinting in the corners of defiant eyes as they proposed both to themselves and to us that "All shall be well." It was an unforgettable version of that questionable benediction, here embracing the irony of its own questionability and rejecting no level of critical nuance. For me the brilliance of the production came into razor-sharp focus at that point. I could never gainsay the power of that conclusion to Act II, whose icy glitter and all but unbearable tenderness almost surpasses that of the opera's end, when all the jesting and fun of the Rustics' play is over and the boy fairies, with Oberon and Titania, prepare to celebrate the sexual union of the "couples three" in their measured, dainty dance upon the knife edge of Britten's profoundly knowing 'innocence'.

While *A Midsummer Night's Dream* is not, as a whole, my favourite Britten opera, it can still sound 'new' and daring. The protestations and exasperations of the adult lovers are set within a kind of ritual or pageant of tintinnabulation that accompanies the boy fairies with quasi-Balinese bells and metallophones that 'place' them somewhere between *Noye's Fludde* and the Venice Lido. It frequently feels almost *avant-garde* in tone and manner (in the context of the period), and possessed of its own judiciously highbrow austerities, in spite of its two quasi-redemptive finales – that is, to Acts II and III specifically. For these alone, I, as a willing middlebrow, will be happy to catch and, yes, be entertained by any performance, any production that comes my way. Western iconography has so long relied upon infant cherubs, *putti* and *amoretti* to bring and represent such blessings as are bestowed, above all, in the Act II finale, that it seems almost like a homage to convention to use unbroken boys' voices to suggest how such cherubs might *sound*, what kind of song we might want them to sing.

Bridcut's reference to what was in "Britten's mind" when conceiving his boy fairies as being far from the conventional "innocent nothings," and possessed of "a kind of sharpness" was drawn, as we have seen, from the essay that the composer himself contributed to the *Observer* a week before the opera's premiere in 1960 and was also included in the programme book for the Alden production. Bridcut glossed Britten's own explanation of what he thought about the fairies by referencing a work closely contemporary with *A Midsummer Night's Dream*, namely the *Missa Brevis* written for George Malcolm's Westminster Cathedral choir in 1958. Their recording (with Malcolm) remains an extraordinary document. In the 'Kyrie' the boys' voices are no less un-innocently possessed of "a kind of sharpness," sounding like hovering flame-spirits conjured in some well-nigh pagan ritual.

Much as I might prefer the *Dream*'s fairies to be visually contextualized in Shakespeare's woods, away from the imprisoning structures of civilization, Alden's production managed to reclaim the danger and the sheer otherness of these outwardly playful and vulnerable schoolboys, for whose movingly questionable benediction at the end of Act II I will periodically forego the grand symphonic sweep and visionary energy of operas like *Peter Grimes* and *Billy Budd*. Perhaps it is to be reminded that they hover in the wings there too, by proxy, just as they would be re-embodied in the wandering, dancing form of Tadzio, pointing nonchalantly towards the horizon and, perhaps, the redemptive, far-sighted sail of Billy and Vere.

Notes

1. Chowrimootoo and Guthrie, Introduction to 'Colloquy: Music and the Middlebrow', 328. They are introducing the term 'Middlebrow' as coined in the 1920s.
2. Richard Taruskin, in Chowrimootoo and Guthrie, 'Colloquy: Music and the Middlebrow', 383.
3. The reminder comes in 'Colloquy: Music and the Middlebrow', 381. Differently paginated in each volume of the *Oxford History of Music*, the quotation will be found almost half way down its fifth page (near the end of the paragraph that begins "But of course semiotics . . .").
4. Taruskin, in Chowrimootoo and Guthrie, 'Colloquy: Music and the Middlebrow', 385.
5. The relevant text is 'Florestan' Shrovetide Oration Delivered after a Performance of Beethoven's Ninth Symphony' (1835). See Henry Pleasants (trans. and ed.), *The Musical World of Robert Schumann: A Selection from His Own Writings* (London: Gollancz, 1965), 31–4.
6. ". . . it is insulting to address anyone in a language they do not understand." – Benjamin Britten, *On Receiving the First Aspen Award* (London: Faber & Faber, 1964), 12.
7. Chowrimootoo and Guthrie, 'Colloquy: Music and the Middlebrow', 328.
8. The specific term Hanslick denies to texted music is *Tonkunst* (strictly, 'art-music' – perhaps a better translation than just "music", as used by both Cohen and Payzant in their translations of the second chapter of Hanslick's 1854 *Vom musikalisch-Schönen*). See Gustav Cohen, *The Beautiful in Music* (Indianapolis: Bobbs-Merrill, 1957 etc), 30 and Geoffrey Payzant, *On the Musically Beautiful* (Indianapolis: Hackett, 1986), 15.
9. Rather than reproducing the texts, for those who do not know them, my hope would be that my description might at the very least prompt the sympathetic reader to seek out a recording, with the texts included.
10. The reference is to Schiller's essay 'Über naïve und sentimentalische Dichtung' (1795–6). The solo trombone passage in the first movement of Mahler's Third Symphony occurs at rehearsal number 33. Interestingly, Hans Keller makes use of, and further elucidates Schiller's distinction between the 'naïve' and the 'sentimental' in the second part of his long 1979 essay 'Operatic Music and Britten' – see Hans Keller, *Britten. Essays, Letters and Opera Guides*, ed. Christopher Wintle and M. Garnham (London: Plumbago Books, 2013), 154–5.
11. Theodor W. Adorno, *Mahler. A Musical Physiognomy*, trans. Edmund Jephcott (Chicago and London: Chicago University Press, 1992), 29. The original German reads "Mütterlich fährt Mahlers Musik, denen, welchen sie sich zuwendet, über die Haare" – Theodor W. Adorno, *Mahler. Eine musikalische Physiognomik* (Frankfurt M.: Suhrkamp, 1960 etc.), 44.
12. See above, 000 [VI (*Teaching opera . . .*) 15] and 2.
13. Gillian Widdicombe, *Observer Review*, Sunday 30 March 1980, Section 3, 33.
14. Eve Kosofsky Sedgewick, *The Epistemology of the Closet*, updated with a new preface (Berkeley, Los Angeles and London: University of California Press, 2008).

15 Donald Mitchell, *Britten and Auden in the Thirties* (London: Faber & Faber, 1981), 154. The song is the first in the 1938 collection *On this Island*.
16 The poem is the third of the 'Twelve Songs' as they appear in W.H. Auden, *Collected Shorter Poems 1927–1957* (London: Faber & Faber, 1960), 88. Auden's first line there uses the indefinite article: "Let a florid music praise . . .".
17 Mitchell, *Britten and Auden in the Thirties*, 155.
18 Ronald Duncan, *Working with Britten. A Personal Memoir* (Devon: The Rebel Press, 1981), 27–8. I should add here that the central part of Duncan's memoir, dealing with the joint creation by him and Britten of *The Rape of Lucretia* is rather better written and contains much that is of interest.
19 Brett, *Music and Sexuality in Britten*, 114 (this essay had also appeared in Solie (ed.), *Musicology and Difference. Gender and Sexuality in Music Scholarship*.
20 Brett, *Music and Sexuality in Britten*, 114.
21 Ibid., 115.
22 Ibid., 72.
23 Ibid., 78.
24 The most detailed analytical study of these chords will be found in Harper-Scott's *Ideology in Britten's Operas*, 157–65.
25 Mitchell, *Britten and Auden in the Thirties*, 161 (this was the first publication of Auden's January 1942 letter to Britten, analysing his character and offering him 'advice' – it concludes on 162).
26 Ibid., 109.
27 Ibid., 112 – the source is provided in Donald Mitchell's essay on Slater in Brett's Handbook on *Benjamin Britten, Peter Grimes* (Cambridge: Cambridge University Press, 1983), 30.
28 Ibid., 113.
29 Ibid.
30 See *Billy Budd*, Act II, scene 3. Vere does not precisely quote the notes, but most of the words of Billy's final peroration, although he omits "that is not fate" after "the far-shining sail".
31 Brett, *Music and Sexuality in Britten*, 116.
32 Ibid., 118.
33 Ibid.
34 ENO programme book for *A Midsummer Night's Dream*, May 2011, 12. The programme also included Britten's own extended essay that he had contributed to the *Observer* a week before the opera's premiere in June 1960, in which he described his conception of Puck as "absolutely amoral and yet innocent". [Programme, 25]. That essay was reprinted in Christopher Palmer (ed.), *The Britten Companion* (London: Faber & Faber, 1984), 177–80 and more recently in Paul Kildea (ed.), *Britten on Music* (Oxford: Oxford University Press, 2003), 186–9.
35 ENO programme book, 13.
36 Bridcut, *Britten's Children*, 146–7; the story had first been aired in Carpenter's biography.

37 This was at the head of the rather harrowing article. ENO programme book, 13–17.
38 Brett, *Music and Sexuality in Britten*, 121.
39 Ibid.
40 ENO programme book, 10. Bridcut again quotes here from Britten's essay on the opera; see Note 34 above and what follows below.

8 Essay

Modernism and Musicology

I finally return, as promised, to J. P. E. Harper-Scott's challenging, unintentionally 'alternative' 2018 contribution to Chowrimootoo's reassessment of Britten. Harper-Scott, following Badiou, invokes the emancipatory Event of Musical Modernism.[1] Much of his language, and that of the theorists he cites, derives from a Marxist-orientated belief in this event as a cherished article of faith. In an earlier essay he had celebrated Alain Badiou's comparison of the authentic modernist revolutionary with Spartacus, whose 'faithful' fellow-slave followers would accept that they must be crucified for their faithfulness, unlike the 'reactive' also-rans who hoped pragmatically to accommodate their Roman masters.[2] I have already characterized the faithful modernists I recall from the 1970s as being, in Harper-Scott's rigorously challenging terms, no less defined by capital than the members of other 'identity' groups effectively mocked by him – and he has some excoriatingly challenging things to say about commodified 'gay identity' that could align him with Britten. I might, however, diabolically ventriloquize the sales pitch of the Devil's department-store manager as my recalled faithful modernists come into view:

> You want to be experimental iconoclasts, challenging conservative conceptions of tonal relationships and musical manners? You'll need some graph-paper from the ground floor, probably a copy of the *I Ching* or Marx's *Capital* from the third floor (the new edition of the former is on offer with a bargain reduction on Cage's *Silence*) – oh, and the black polo-neck sweaters you'll find just over there.

'Faithful subjects' of musical modernism in the 1970s had their own identity and were vulnerable to precisely the sort of critical deconstruction that Harper-Scott had applied to those aspiring to *gay* identity. The implications of this failed to nuance his earlier, but highly relevant, critique of Britten's supposedly 'conventional' opposition – in *Death in Venice* – of dissonant atonal (or even serial) writing to the conventionally 'safe' tonal order into which it is ultimately "brought back".[3] I ventured earlier (see p. 64.) that Britten might have used serially organized dissonance in a quasi-ironic manner,

DOI: 10.4324/9781032666631-8

that the original story consistently *ironized* Aschenbach's perception of himself in ways that were linked to Mann's variously delicate and sometimes comic ways of presenting decadent aesthetes, artists and Wagnerians (rather like himself) in stories and novels from *Buddenbrooks* onwards. Nervously disposed modernists would exasperatedly spot the way in which Britten will space and orchestrally colour conventionally 'dissonant' chords to sound as memorably, *consumably* impressive as those that characterize the pompous pride of the hotel manager. This fateful "stranger" (a term Harper-Scott borrows from Lloyd Whitesell[4]) actually proves more of a shape-shifting *insider* in the opera, and dissonance serves eloquent rhetorical ends as he welcomes the real stranger, Aschenbach, to the Lido and the Grand Hotel before extolling the view of the sea – at which bracingly inviting gusts of tonal air blow in from the beach in Act I, Scene 4. The fact that Aschenbach reacts to it all in a kind of deliberately distancing, 'literary' second hand is surely a clearer source of the 'corruption' the opera deals with than the truth of Tadzio's beauty.[5]

There is one revealing, indeed disappointing aspect of Harper-Scott's theoretical weaponizing of his otherwise highly interesting and complex readings of Britten's operatic 'ideology', challengingly elaborated in his 2018 book. This is his rather dreary wheeling in of the arch music-analytical ideologue Heinrich Schenker. What *can* we do with Schenker's 'voice-leading graphs' other than admire their effortfully, surreptitiously deceitful construction? The deceit was ever implicit in the elaborately tendentious edifice of Schenker's 'system', designed to *prove* that Great Works of the Germanic tonal tradition were 'great' because the 'greatness' of their composers was revealed in their (supposedly?) ideologically neutral unfolding of tonal arguments over time. Their works' apparently demonstrable "organic unity" arose from inspired "improvisation" – which was as close as human subjects (a significant proportion of whom Schenker believed to be irretrievably "unmusical"[6]) could be expected to get to truly organic nature in the activity of "inspired" creation. This was a philosophical illusionist's trick that Schenker performed threateningly for modernists and Wagnerians who thought they could change the nature of Truth (and consequently the Truth of Nature?). In post-Wagnerian composition, based on Wagner's example, the foregrounded and theoretically mediated motivic technique, Schenker proclaimed, failed to "attain the breadth and expanse of improvisation . . ."

> which alone creates the organic structure of sonata form. A tradition of sonata form is entirely lacking. How could it ever have arisen when the general musical opinion as well as the general instinct was unable to cope with exactly that characteristic, the intuitive, improvisational process which unites the parts of the form by means of progressions? The sonata form of the masters, however, will remain preserved for all time by virtue of the integrity of the improvisational style.[7]

In other words, the masters renounce intentional mastery by relying on their divinely gifted intuitive genius.

* * *

We might, at this point, confront more directly the later unfolding of Harper-Scott's approach in *Ideology in Britten's Operas*, precisely contemporary as it chanced to be with Chowrimootoo's *Middlebrow Modernism*. While grounded upon the insights and arguments put forward in 'Britten and the Deadlock of Identity Politics', and arguably sharing some of the problems I have attempted to highlight in relation to that essay, I am nonetheless bound to characterize the more recent book as a challengingly serious and unquestionably significant contribution. It could indeed give rise to an extended study in its own right, and not least in its aspect, highlighted in my Foreword, as a kind of professional 'suicide note'. In 2021 Harper-Scott assumed in reverse the role of the evil Fairy Carabosse who, in the first act of Tchaikovsky's ballet *The Sleeping Beauty*, storms in, uninvited, upon Princess Aurora's christening to place her prophetic curse upon the child. Instead, Harper-Scott chose, no less dramatically or publicly, to sweep *out of* musicology and his university post, apparently to take up an entirely new career, leaving behind him a kind of retrospective curse upon his discipline, on grounds that would already have been clear enough to any diligent reader of *Ideology in Britten's Operas*.[8] Throughout the book we encounter the elements of a Marxian critique of the neoliberal capitalist academy, with its positioning of students as 'consumers' of an educational 'experience' delivered by bureaucratically managed scholars who are required not only to cater to student needs and 'preferences' but also to be producing a set annual number of 'outputs' like intellectual commodities.

There is much in what he says, but, like his old-fashioned equation of the modernist musical event with Schoenberg (whose Second String Quartet of 1908 is cited as providing evidence of the fabled "emancipation of dissonance" without taking account of its quietly radiant and entirely consonant conclusion in F sharp major[9]), his stern-sounding insistence that music students' experience should be subordinated to their necessary transformation into "intellectual apprentices who need to submit to the discipline of internalizing a body of knowledge and method" digs him a little deeper into a traditionalist trench.[10] And once the students have thus submitted, he is careful to explain that what they will be studying are "artworks as opposed to pieces of entertainment."[11] Not for him the 'postmodern' levelled playing field on which he locates film music, and other genres in which the art-form is, he tells us, no more than an "alienated", "subordinate" prettification of consumer-orientated products geared to "conventional emotional release" of the kind that will ensnare us in "the ideology of capitalism."[12]

It is not difficult to mock the rather traditional, old-musicological ways that seem to attach themselves like cherished barnacles to the hull of this otherwise well-armed vessel that is mapping dangerous and uncharted waters of musical meaning. There is nevertheless much to admire in the passionate, albeit often angry, sincerity of Harper-Scott's powerful critical analyses of the operas he chooses to concentrate on. Initially it is *Owen Wingrave*; but others follow, and most significantly, perhaps, *Billy Budd* in the hundred-page essay on the opera that forms Part II of his book ('The Ship of State'). Here Edward Fairfax Vere is angrily demoted to a weak and cowardly victim of ideologically driven confusion. Subsequently, in a movingly complex final chapter, he concentrates on *Curlew River*, latterly in relation to *Death in Venice*, and the composer's dialectical inspiration by Japanese musical and dramatic manners.[13] Like Chowrimootoo, Harper-Scott – nervously anxious to insist on analysing "the notes" – pays careful attention to the interaction and contrast between serially organized and more obviously tonal textures, but less crudely opposed as 'faithful' modernism and 'reactive' or even 'obscure' tonal 'sentiment' (in the manner of Chowrimootoo); he has, of course, also to add heterophony to the mix when treating the later operas.

There remain the old-style 'analytical' passages of intricate harmonic examination of key and even specific note significance (I can occasionally imagine Britten politely congratulating Harper-Scott and adding – obfuscatorily? – "I'm sure I could never have *planned* all that."). There is one delicious moment where an exquisitely complex and typographically elaborate full-page voice-leading reduction of Act II of *The Rape of Lucretia* is introduced almost flippantly:

> A glance at Figure 5.5 . . . will sufficiently demonstrate the means by which the B becomes the 'stain' on Lucretia's chastity.[14]

A *glance*? The chart surely merits framing and exhibiting in a Museum of Aesthetic Mystification. Such things are meant elegantly to crush and overawe the common reader, and not a few musicological ones (it must have taken hours to formulate). Of course it demonstrates nothing but what you *believe* it demonstrates. No mere glance will inspire faith.

For all the estimable if sometimes compromised analytical work on display here, Harper-Scott has more to offer. He clearly grasps that to support his mercilessly harsh, often bitter interpretation of Vere's responsibility for not preventing Billy's hanging at the end of *Billy Budd*, it will be necessary to talk about the historical situation that would have conditioned the psychology of the main characters in their roles on *The Indomitable* as a miniature 'ship of state'. He points out that the opera's cited mutinies at Spithead and The Nore were barely 'mutinies' at all (being largely non-violent) and that Vere's closing peroration may truly represent no resolution. I would nevertheless question his use of the term 'tranquillizing' when approaching things that Chowrimootoo would likely just call "sentimental."[15] Harper-Scott recoils at all moments of engagement that put the listener in a state receptive to ideological manipulation or 'interpellation', moments relevant to my broader notion of 'entertainment' (another term that merits careful unpacking) of the kind that Britten himself explicitly sought to offer his listeners.[16] But I am convinced and indeed impressed by Harper-Scott's *own* vulnerable and quasi-redemptive peroration at the end of his Part II *Billy Budd* essay, where he adds an odd, defensive 'merely' to this attempt both to divine and ostensibly decry any real transcendence, in Britten's operas, of their own socio-ideological historicity:

> they merely outline – with terrifying clarity, and in music of exceptional power and inventive intelligence – exactly how difficult it is, given the scale of the systemic violence which holds it in place, to make any inroads at all in a cultural struggle for an ideological shift.[17]

I may not wholly *believe* in his readings (including those of parts of *Peter Grimes*, *The Rape of Lucretia* and *The Turn of the Screw*), but the engagement and powerful sincerity of the concluding lines of his remarkable study fashion a determinedly resonant 'last' musicological word (if such it is). Returning to the importance of "critical thinking and listening," he suggests that it might

> lead on to a genuine redrawing of our ideological boundaries. The hope is small, but the promise of a world we can barely see, in which human beings can dwell once more, should be enough to help those who reject the false equivalences of postmodernism to discover, think through, commit to, and ultimately proclaim what they faithfully believe to be true.

* * *

In the fun park of relatively recent musicology, my search for any comfortingly firm ground on which to base my own nervously ventured convictions and esteem for Britten appears fruitless. Musicology has become something like a cross between a roller coaster, a ghost train and a hall of mirrors, not least as I seek, for example, to find support for my disbeliever's questioning of Schenker's role in Harper-Scott's larger project. I might, however, return to the late Richard Taruskin who, in one of the pieces in his 2009 collection *The Danger of Music and Other Anti-Utopian Essays*, characterized Schenker as

> the Great Austrian music theorist who was frankly antagonistic toward modern music and hence more literally devoted than any of the modernists to the defense and preservation of the German classical tradition. Like Schoenberg before his exile, Schenker was at once a Jew and a fanatical German suprematist. He died in 1935, before the Anschluss, and therefore never had to experience Webern's tragic disillusionment. But even taking all of that into account, the rabid identification with Hitler he revealed in a letter he sent one of his pupils in May 1933 verges on the unbelievable.[18]

Here Taruskin surely landed an unintended direct hit on this particular weak point in Harper-Scott's armour. The latter has admittedly acknowledged Schenker's "diatribes against the faithful-modernist music of his time,"[19] but appeared to overlook his forcefully expressed support for the Führer – and all this in Harper-Scott's now-notorious 2012 *Quilting-Points* study of modernism whose first thirty-odd pages take the form of a Taruskinian, no-holds-barred attack *on* Taruskin himself, denounced as an anti-European, anti-*British* American spokesman for "global neoliberal capitalism."[20] Evidence of this, Harper-Scott suggests, was to be found in Taruskin's opposition of 'pleasure and enjoyment' to Julian Johnson's moralizing about the depth and ethical necessity of "'great' art and music"[21] that resists egalitarianism in favour of "fundamental human aspiration."[22] One of Johnson's more haughty pronouncements was as follows:

> The demand that composers should say what they have to say in a more accessible language, however well meant, betrays a signal lack of understanding about art.[23]

Not surprisingly, Britten (who warmly embraced such a 'misunderstanding' in his Aspen Award speech) makes no appearance in the Index of Johnson's *Who Needs Classical Music? Cultural Choice and Musical Value*. Of other twentieth-century composers, Schoenberg has eight entries, Stravinsky six, Boulez and Berg two each, Varèse one.

In truth, Harper-Scott's extended critique of Taruskin's two *Oxford History* volumes dealing with the twentieth century is a powerful tirade. He rather convincingly analyses those volumes' unfolding and xenophobically biassed, USA-centred account of the trumping of European modernism by American new music after the USA-USSR stand-off of the Cold War. It would have to be a brave soul who would dare to question his interpretation of how and where Taruskin pins *his* quilting points in order to structure and manage the "flow of signifiers" in his account (meaning guiding concepts like 'maximalism', which reveal the ideological strategy of his telling of history). I certainly breathe a sigh of relief to find my own work consistently ignored by Harper-Scott, not least in view of the evidence of a level of mutual sympathy between myself and the late Professor Taruskin, in whose Berkeley department I was privileged to work for a few months in 2010, already formulating the suspicion that 'faithful modernism' *was itself* the most significantly problematic 'quilting point' in conventional narratives of the history of twentieth-century European music. But we are still in the hall of mirrors, and as we shall see, Taruskin publicly confirmed his support of Chowrimootoo's *Middlebrow Modernism*.[24] This puts me in an even more ambivalently awkward position; I certainly sense the red laser spot of the cop-show gangster's gun aim on my back as I read Harper-Scott's Footnote 4, in which he scorns 'aesthetic questions' of taste (as in truth do I) and attributes them to "dilettantism," depending on a personal 'sense', gained through many years of privileged exposure to a range of artefacts, which is meant to be respected simply because as evidence of experience it surpasses that of ordinary mortals.[25]

Well, I am at least prepared to deny any claim on 'respect' and consider myself quite as 'ordinary' as Harper-Scott.

The musicological roller coaster's next sudden dip, in this brief summary, as it hurtles perhaps back down towards Harper-Scott, comes when we consider how boldly Taruskin indeed publicized his support for Chowrimootoo's approach to Britten in *Middlebrow Modernism*. That statement appeared in the 'Colloquy, Musicology and the Middlebrow' in the *Journal of the American Musicological Society*, Summer 2020, where he revealed that

> it fell to me to defend Chowrimootoo's *Middlebrow Modernism. Britten's Operas and the Great Divide* against a blackballing prepublication referee. The book uses the category of the middlebrow as a heuristic through which to expose several decades' worth of false consciousness embodied in reviews of Britten's stage works. Britten, ostensibly the subject of the book, serves more as a catalyst, somewhat in the way he did for me in *The Oxford History of Western Music*, which juxtaposes chapters on Britten and Elliott Carter to exemplify what I called the mid-twentieth-century 'standoff'. . . . Britten engaged both high aestheticist and communitarian credence. He liked to emphasize the latter in his public utterances, knowing that he had reliable spokespersons to advance the former, often pre-emptively. His work provided a place where critics could actually do what Virginia Woolf always feared the middlebrow might do, "saying one thing and doing the opposite, indulging base desires while laying claim to aesthetic purity." Chowrimootoo's book caught them, delectably, in *flagrante*. But the word 'middlebrow'. . . blinded our referee to the book's point and purpose and came across as an attack on Britten. . . . I managed to counter this misunderstanding.[26]

Had we read the same book? I hasten to add that I was not the "blackballing critic" – although I might have been, and have regretfully perhaps made up for that omission in the present study. Is it really the *critics* Chowrimootoo catches *in flagrante*, or is it not ever more explicitly *Britten himself*? I confess I take it to be the latter throughout, guided by that initial and clear attribution of "sickly sentimentality" to *Peter Grimes*. Indulging base desires while laying claim to aesthetic purity appears to be what Chowrimootoo confesses to at the outset of his book – thus catching *himself* "in flagrante"?

Paradoxically, it is Taruskin who reveals the potential for a contrasting, healthier (if still wary) sympathy with that opera in reference to the Act II female quartet. Chowrimootoo is snaring no unsuspecting 'critic' when *he* makes a significant observation about that quartet, entirely off his own bat (as we say in benighted, no longer 'European', old England). I referred at the beginning of Chapter 5 to his discovery of an extreme response to *Der Rosenkavalier* in a novel – a response which actually matched Britten's own. The relevant passage in Iris Murdoch's *The Black Prince* concluded with the scornful Bradley Pearson mocking "opera's 'cheap' thrills and mindless entertainment" in a rather general way. Writing about *Peter Grimes*, Chowrimootoo is more specific:

> The Act II women's quartet bears a striking resemblance to Strauss's *Rosenkavalier* Trio and Ellen could easily be described as the Borough's "melodious Mimi": every time she opens her mouth, we hear luscious strings, angelic harps and sumptuous lyricism that seems to halt the dramatic action.[27]

Another 'silly operatic woman' for Chowrimootoo, then? Who indeed is once more caught *in flagrante* here? This, by way of contrast, is Taruskin on *Grimes*, Act II, in the notorious *Oxford History*:

> The climax comes when the whole town (excepting Ellen and Balstrode) shout the charge of "Murder!" to the strident inversion of the ninth in which Grimes had rested all his hope.
> All rush off, but for a quartet of women, who remain alone onstage and sing one of the opera's famous set pieces, a pained commentary on the harsh life of the fishing community and the toll it takes on mortals – a commentary given added ironic point by being sung, apart from Ellen, by the innkeeper ("Auntie") and her "nieces", the girls she keeps to provide the men of the town with comfort services: three women, in other words, identified by hypocritical convention as immoral, but alone (with Ellen) exhibiting a humanity which the town's more respectable citizens have been exposed as lacking.[28]

There is more, and he is good on the quartet's "dissonant ritornello" which, he tells us, has been compared with "the voices of seagulls supplementing the rocking waves of the sea."[29] Remove the self-conscious, self-protective "one of the opera's famous set pieces" and the insistence on "irony," but add a gentle reminder to the (sadly late) alpha male musicologist that these women are singing specifically *about men* and their childlike ways, and you have here the outline of a response that strikes me as sensitive and germane to the dramatic issue. Nothing of that touches the modernist austerity of Chowrimootoo, jealously guarding himself from infection by sentimentality.

Much is revealed of us in the words we use to describe our experiences, musical ones perhaps most of all. Nervousness about doing so used to express itself in the formulae of "purely musical" assurances that "no words can express." But they can and we must try to find them, if we care, accepting that their censure served to protect male listeners above all from revealing to what extent music "comforted" them – as the nieces comfort the fishermen of the Borough or as Grimes is comforted by the thought that one day all might be well and that he might marry Ellen. In their "set piece" quartet, led by Auntie and Ellen, the women grasp and embrace all the needs of fallen, fallible men (even musicologists) in pitying, perhaps transcendent love, beyond all irony and dissembling:

> Do we smile or shall we weep
> Or wait quietly till they sleep?

Notes

1. I refer here, of course, to Harper-Scott, *Ideology in Britten's Operas*. His complex explanation of the non-time-bound 'Event' is specifically linked to the *"emancipation of dissonance"* (Harper-Scott's emphasis) on 106.
2. Harper-Scott explains Badiou's use of Spartacus and his Roman slave army in his 2013 essay 'Britten and the Deadlock of Identity Politics', in Philip Purvis (ed.), *Masculinity in Opera. Gender, History and New Musicology* (New York and London: Routledge, 2013), 155.
3. See J.P.E. Harper-Scott, 'Britten and the Deadlock of Identity Politics', 156.
4. Ibid., 152.
5. See Ibid., 158; here Harper-Scott oddly and rather primly refers to the "corrupting effects of Tadzio, the beautiful fourteen-year-old boy" – perhaps an inadvertent example of 'blaming the victim'?
6. In the Introduction to *Der freie Satz*, Schenker claimed that "It is certain that almost half of mankind is unmusical, even incapable of singing a folk tune . . .". See Heinrich Schenker, *Free Composition (Der freie Satz), Vol. III of New Musical Theories and Fantasies*, trans. Ernst Oster (New York and London: Longman, 1979), Introduction, xxiv.
7. Heinrich Schenker, 'Organic Structure in Sonata Form' in Maury Yeston (ed.), *Readings in Schenker Analysis and Other Approaches*, trans. Orin Grossman (New Haven and London: Yale University Press, 1977), 53.
8. The full text of Harper-Scott's 'Why I left academia' appeared on his website (jpehs.co.uk) in September 2021; accessed by the present author on 21 July 21 via: https://jpehs.co.uk/why-i-left-academia/?mc_cid=f8ee6c503b&mc_eid=7f30380895.
9. Harper-Scott, *Ideology in Britten's Operas*, 106.
10. Ibid., 44.
11. Ibid., 25.
12. Ibid., 12.
13. Harper-Scott's highly idealized treatment of Japanese culture, overlooking the shadow of violence its undoubtedly impressive and alluring philosophical and aesthetic achievements occlude, is a touchingly vulnerable characteristic of the later stage of his argument here.
14. Harper-Scott, *Ideology in Britten's Operas*, 209.

15 Harper-Scott's use of the word "tranquillizing" (for example, with reference to the last group of "interview chords", Ibid., 161) relates to his Brechtian disapproval of the supposedly intellectually "anaesthetizing" effect of popular forms of entertainment outlined early in *Ideology in Britten's Operas* (eg. 8–9). A later scornful reference to ideological "outsider anxiety", illustrated with reference to "any John Wayne or *Independence Day*-style film" (142) leads me to suspect that if he could overcome his distaste for mass-entertainment cinema, he would be an informed and discerning critic of it.
16 See Britten, *On Receiving the First Aspen Award*, 12: '. . . I can find nothing wrong with offering to my fellow-men music which may inspire them or comfort them, which may touch them or entertain them . . .".
17 Harper-Scott, *Ideology in Britten's Operas*, 171.
18 Richard Taruskin, *The Danger of Music and Other Anti-Utopian Essays* (Berkeley, Lo Angeles and London: University of California Press, 2009), 211. Taruskin goes on here to quote the mentioned letter of Schenker's that began: "The historical achievement of Hitler, the extermination of Marxism, will be celebrated by posterity . . .".
19 I refer here to J.P.E. Harper-Scott, *The Quilting Points of Musical Modernism. Revolution, Reaction and William Walton* (Cambridge: Cambridge University Press, 2012), 201.
20 Ibid., 18.
21 Julian Johnson, *Who Needs Classical Music? Cultural Choice and Musical Value* (Oxford: Oxford University Press, 2002), 17.
22 Ibid., 113.
23 Ibid., 104. Harper-Scott's treatment of Julian Johnson's book, specifically as attacked by Taruskin in a famous review of it, will be found in his *Quilting Points*, 13–17, where he cites the Taruskin review as reprinted in Taruskin, *The Danger of Music and Other Anti-Utopian Essays*, as 'The Musical Mystique. Defending Classical Music against Its Devotees', 330–53 (it also covers books by Joshua Fineberg and Lawrence Kramer).
24 See below (and note 26).
25 Harper-Scott, *The Quilting Points*, xi.
26 Chowrimootoo and Guthrie, 'Colloquy: Music and the Middlebrow', 380–1. Taruskin credits the internal quotation from Woolf to Chowrimootoo's *Middlebrow Modernism*, 14.
27 Chowrimootoo. *Middlebrow Modernism*, 51. The previous reference is to Murdoch's novel *The Black Prince* as discussed by Chowrimootoo: Ibid., 147–8. It might be noted that Harper-Scott reduces Ellen to a functional role as a "patriarchal cipher in support of a male character" (*Ideology in Britten's Operas*, 203).
28 Taruskin, *Music in the Late Twentieth Century*, 240.
29 Taruskin, Ibid., 240.

Select Bibliography

Given the ever-expanding literature available on Britten, and in the interests of economy, this Select Bibliography does not reproduce all the references listed in the Endnotes, but concentrates on key resources and books engaged with in the text and recommended as essential reading for those seeking to explore further the arguments I have put forward. Those seeking more conventional or extended stylistic analysis of works discussed might consult Peter Evans, *The Music of Benjamin Britten*, revised edn. 1979 (London: Dent, 1989) or Arnold Whittall, *The Music of Britten and Tippett: Studies in Themes and Techniques* (Cambridge: Cambridge University Press 1982).

Brett, Philip. *Music and Sexuality in Britten. Selected Essays*, ed. George E. Haggerty (Berkeley, Los Angeles and London: University of California Press, 2006).

Carpenter, Humphrey. *Benjamin Britten: A Biography* (London: Faber & Faber, 1992).

Chowrimootoo, Christopher. *Middlebrow Modernism. Britten's Opera and the Great Divide* (Oakland, California: University of California Press, 2018).

——— with Kate Guthrie (convenors). 'Colloquy: Musicology and the Middlebrow', *Journal of the American Musicological Society*, Vol. 72, 2 (Summer 2020).

Harper-Scott, J.P.E. *Ideology in Britten's Operas* (Cambridge: Cambridge University Press, 2018).

Mellers, Wilfrid. *Caliban Reborn. Renewal in Twentieth-Century Music* (London: Victor Gollancz Ltd., 1968).

Mitchell, Donald. *Britten and Auden in the Thirties* (London: Faber & Faber, 1981).

Purvis, Philip (ed.). *Masculinity in Opera. Gender, History and New Musicology* (New York and London: Routledge 2013).

Rupprecht, Philip. *Britten's Musical Language* (Cambridge: Cambridge University Press, 2001).

Solie, Ruth (ed.). *Musicology and Difference. Gender and Sexuality in Music Scholarship* (Berkeley, Los Angeles and London: University of California Press, 1993).

Taruskin, Richard. *The Danger of Music and Other Anti-Utopian Essays* (Berkeley, Los Angeles and London: University of California Press, 2009).
Taruskin, Richard. *Music in the Late Twentieth Century, Vol. 5 of The Oxford History of Western Music* (Oxford: Oxford University Press, 2010).
Wiebe, Heather. *Britten's Unquiet Pasts. Sound and Memory in Postwar Reconstruction* (Cambridge: Cambridge University Press, 2012/15), 1.

Acknowledgements

Warmest thanks are due to my friends Charlotte Purkis, who provided invaluable support throughout, and Robert Gibson, who read the manuscript and was discriminatingly enthusiastic. Heidi Bishop at Routledge was ever encouraging and my anonymous readers both supportive and constructive in their suggestions. I also acknowledge a debt to the late Professor Richard Taruskin, with whom this book is often in subterranean conversation.

Index

Adler, Guido vii, 34, 69, 86
Adorno, Theodor 4, 58, 84, 97n11
Albert Herring 40
Aldeburgh 8, 25, 47, 48, 51, 52, 54–5, 59, 70, 72
Alden, Christopher 92–6
Analysis (musical) vii 86, 101–3
Aspen Award, The (and Britten's speech) 80, 109n16
Aston, Peter 31, 54–5, 66n1
Auden, W. H. 81, 85–6, 90, 95, 98n16, 98n25

BBC, The 4, 22, 48, 51, 57
Beatles, The 7, 15, 48, 51
Beethoven 1, 3, 7, 32, 48, 97n5
Berg, Alban 15, 105
Berlin (East) 68–9, 95
Billy Budd 27, 48–50, 57, 71, 88–9, 96, 98n30
Billy Budd, Sailor (Melville) 90
Blake, David 30–1, 44n3, 46, 52, 57, 68–9
Blake, William 27, 83
Boulez, Pierre 3, 15, 32, 40, 51, 79, 105
Brain, Denis 78
Brecht, Berthold 52–3n7, 109n15
Brett, Philip 20, 39, 45n24, 59, 66, 85, 87–8, 90–1, 95
Bridcut, John 43n1, 94–6
Burgess and Maclean 90
Byrd, William 55, 66n1

Cage, John 3, 15, 48, 79, 100
Carpenter, Humphrey 7, 34, 85, 98n36
Chowrimootoo, Christopher viii–ix, 4–8, 17–20, 22–3, 30, 33–8, 40, 49, 50, 57–9, 62–6, 72, 78–8, 83, 90, 95, 100, 102–3, 105–8
Class 1, 6–8, 17, 79–80
'Classical Music' 1, 3–4, 80
Coleman, Basil 19–20
Cooke, Deryck 57, 58
Cooke, Mervyn 22, 48
Crabbe, George 39, 41
Crozier, Eric 94
Culshaw, John 25
Curlew River 103

Death in Venice 56, 57–66, 72, 74, 75, 85, 90, 96, 100–01, 103
Debussy, Claude 15, 48
Delius, Frederick 4
Dream of Gerontius, The 74
Duncan, Ronald 87, 98n18

Elgar, Sir Edward 2, 5, 74
English National Opera 50, 52n5, 58, 92
'Englishness' 4
English Opera Group 60

Faber & Faber 70, 86
Fischer-Dieskau, Dietrich 23
Franck, César 16, 47

Index

Gloriana 90
Guthrie, Kate 34, 78, 79, 80, 97n1

Handel, George Frideric 16
Hanslick, Eduard 82, 97n8
Harper-Scott, J. P. E. viii–ix, 4–5, 20, 90, 98n24, 100–06, 108n1, 108n2, 108n5, 108n8, 108n13, 109n15, 109n23
Heath, Sir Edward 60, 69
Hitler, Adolf 104–5, 109n18
Holloway, Robin 5
Holst, Gustav 2
Holst, Imogen 55
Hymn to St Cecelia 16, 46, 54

James, Henry 18
Johnson, Julian 105, 109n23

Keats, John 84
Keller, Hans 97n10
Kildea, Paul 14n18
Knepler, Georg 68–9
Knot Garden, The 58
Koltai, Ralph 58
Komische Oper 68–9

Leavis, F. R. 35, 47
Ledger, Philip 25
Leeds 85–6
'Let the florid music' 85–6
Lied von der Erde, Das 86–7
Listener, The 72

Mahler, Alma 51–2, 70
Mahler, Gustav 3, 21–2, 23, 25, 42–3, 50–2, 54, 56–7, 62–3, 70, 73, 76–7, 83–4, 86–7
Malcolm, George 96
Mann, Thomas 58, 61, 63–4
Mann, William 47
Marx, Karl 36, 39, 100, 102
Mayer, Sir Robert 16–17
McClary, Susan 6
Mellers, Wilfrid 3, 6–7, 13n11, 15, 25, 30, 32, 41, 43, 46, 47–8, 50–1, 52
Melodrama 18

Melville, Herman 90
Messiaen, Olivier 46
Middle-/ Highbrow 6–7, 13n9, 17–18, 33–5, 36–8, 47–8, 50, 78–81, 97n1, 105–6
Midsummer Night's Dream, A (Britten) 25, 69, 90–6
Missa Brevis 16, 96
Mitchell, Donald 52, 56–7, 61, 69–70, 72, 76–7, 85–7
Modernism 3–8, 17–18, 34, 36–7, 40–1, 63–4, 79–80, 100–01, 104–8
Moore, Henry 32
Morris, William 50, 52n6
Mozart 16, 21
Murdoch, Iris 34, 107, 109n27

New Statesman, The 5, 6
Nolan, Sidney 56
Noyes Fludde 8–9, 10–12, 15, 23–4, 43, 96

On This Island see 'Let the Florid Music'
Owen, Wilfred 23, 24–5
Owen Wingrave 8, 51, 57, 103

Palmer, Christopher 15
Palmer, Tony 75, 85
Paul Bunyan 41–2, 81
Pears, Peter 23, 25, 30–2, 33–4, 39–40, 41, 46–7, 54–6, 60 2, 72–3, 75–7, 78, 85, 90
Peter Grimes 4–5, 8, 15, 27–30, 33–4, 35, 36–43, 48, 50, 54, 56, 57, 71–2, 85, 87, 96, 104, 106–8
Phaedra 77
Piper, John 19–20, 48, 59, 73–5
Piper, Myfanwy 63, 74
Poet's Echo, The 33
'Popular Music' 1, 3–4
Puccini, Giacomo 2, 38, 40, 71
Punch and Judy (Birtwistle) 57
Purcell 40

Rape of Lucretia, The 87, 103–4
Rejoice in the Lamb 15, 46, 54

Richards, I. A. 35–6
Rigoletto 21, 25, 70
Ring cycle (Wagner) 58, 71
Rite of Spring, The 80
Romeo & Juliet (Tchaikovsky) 16, 21
Rosenkavalier, Der 33–4, 44n6, 51, 107
Rostropovich 30–1
Royal Albert Hall, The 2, 21
Rupprecht, Philip viii, 8, 12

Sadlers Wells 16–17 18–20, 27–30, 38, 58, 60
Schenker, Heinrich 101–2, 103, 104–5, 108n6, 108n18
Schoenberg, Arnold 3, 15, 43, 69, 79–80, 102, 104–5
Schubert, Franz 33, 46–7, 75–6
Sedgwick, Eve Kosovsky 85, 90
Semele (Handel) 16, 21
Sentiment/ality 2, 4–5, 6–7, 8, 18, 23, 24, 33, 35, 36–7, 39, 41, 49, 62, 64, 72, 80, 83, 103, 106, 107
Serenade for Tenor, Horn & Strings 7, 76, 78, 81–4
Shakespeare 4, 17, 91–2, 95
Shepherd, W. Anthony 8
Sherlaw Johnson, Robert 27, 31, 46
Shostakovich, Dmitry 3, 51, 53n8
Sibelius, Jean 3, 6
Six Hölderlin Fragments 33
Slater, Montagu 39, 41, 45n25, 90
Sleeping Beauty, The (Tchaikovsky) 102
Snape, The Maltings 55–6
Solti, Georg 48
Spence, Basil 22
St Nicolas 15–16, 73
Stockhausen, Karlheinz 3, 51, 70, 79
Strauss, Richard 3, 33–4, 51, 71, 77
Stravinsky, Igor 3, 16, 22–3, 26n10, 51, 105
String Quartet no.3 77
Symphony of Psalms (Stravinsky) 16, 51

Tallis, Thomas 12, 66n1
Taruskin, Richard 78–80, 104–7
Tchaikovsky, Piotr Il'yich 2, 16, 21, 102
Tennyson, Baron Alfred 83
Thomson, Rita 73
A Time there Was (film) 75, 85
Tippett, Michael 5, 58, 72
Tristan (Wagner) 15
Turandot (Puccini) 38
Turn of the Screw, The 16–20, 27, 43, 50, 59, 60, 87–8, 90, 91, 95, 104

Vaughan Williams 4, 5–6, 12n1, 15
Venice 62, 63
Verdi, Giuseppe 21, 24, 40, 70
Vienna vii 43
Visconti, Luchino 58–9
Vyvyan, Jennifer 19–20

Wagner, Richard 3, 15, 46, 50–1, 58, 71, 74, 101
Walton, Sir William 6
War Requiem 22–5, 26n10, 30, 54, 91
Webern 15, 104
Weill, Kurt 3
Welsh, Moray 30–1, 43n2, 44n3, 44n4, 44n5, 47
Wiebe, Heather 4, 8
Williams, Raymond 27, 35–7, 44n17
Wilson, Harold 60, 70
Winterreise (Schubert) 46–7
Woolf, Virginia 106
Wozzeck (Berg) 15, 17, 37, 50

Yeats, W. B. 20
York 3, 7, 8, 13n13, 15, 25, 27, 30–3, 41, 43, 46–7, 50–2, 54, 56–7, 59, 65–6, 68, 70, 79, 85, 87
Young Person's Guide to the Orchestra, The 3
'Youth and Music' 16–17

For Product Safety Concerns and Information please contact our EU representative GPSR@taylorandfrancis.com
Taylor & Francis Verlag GmbH, Kaufingerstraße 24, 80331 München, Germany

www.ingramcontent.com/pod-product-compliance
Lightning Source LLC
Chambersburg PA
CBHW051754230426
43670CB00012B/2282